Cantina COCKTAILS

Desert Dream, Desert Romance

THE HISTORY, STYLE & FOOD OF ROYAL PALMS RESORT AND SPA

SECOND EDITION

Royal Palms Resort and Spa - History, Style, & Food was written by Robert Z. Chew with photography by Robert Isacson. Production management and recipe editing by Rich Heineck. Recipe testing by Gwen Walters. Project management by Nancy White. Recipes by Executive Chef Lee Hillson and Executive Pastry Chef Pierino Jermonti (desserts).

Published by Royal Palms Resort and Spa
5200 East Camelback Road
Phoenix, Arizona 85018
602.840.3610

ISBN 978-0-9725653-1-8

Produced by:
PFI Communications and PFI/Heineck
Los Angeles, California and Scottsdale, Arizona
323.634.7700

Design by:
Visual i Design, Cathy Gerstmann
Prescott Valley, Arizona
928.830.2135

Printed in China

Photography:
All new color photography by Robert Isacson with the exceptions of page 18 by Mark Alexander; pages 48-49 by J.T. Heineck; pages 68 and 101-105 by Dino Tonn; page 104 by Scott Baxter; pages 78, 82, 85, 125, 132 and 149 by Reddie Henderson; pages 127 and 134 by Al Payne; pages 132 and 135 by Kevin Syms and page 130 by Stacy Lacombe and William Kohn. Historical photography on pages 7-13 and page 15 from the Arizona State Library, Archives and Public Records, Archives Division, Phoenix, 94-7383. Various historical photos pages 32-47 are from the private collections of Fred Renker, Fred and Jennifer Unger, Don Ziebell, Jonathan Dreier, and Jill Alanko. The photo of Chauncey on page 20 was offered from Sally and Robert Overgaard, the grand niece of Florence Cooke.

The Author:
Robert Z. Chew is the author of three non-fiction books, including *Golf in Hollywood: Where the Stars Come Out to Play* (Angel City Press). Chew's second novel, *Jazz and the Atom Bomb* is expected to be released shortly. He lives in Los Angeles and Colorado.

The Photographer:
For the last nineteen years, Robert Isacson has been an award-winning photographer, having earned national recognition for his distinctive style and polished images. Expertly proficient in architectural, commercial, and fashion photography, Robert maintains a studio outside of Washington D.C., but can often be seen throughout the U.S. photographing exquisite properties.

Inside Front Cover: Royal Palms from the early 1960's. Inside Back Cover: An aerial view of the property from the mid 1950's.

Majestic palm trees line the driveway. These were planted in the 1920's when Royal Palms was a winter residence for Delos Cooke.

Contents

A perfect entry.
Turquoise mahogany doors and
Moorish influenced reflecting pool
are original features dating back to
the 1920's when the property was
a private residence.

*"The Hohokam Indians
knew how to make
water dance in the desert."*

An Ancient Land Flowers

Royal Palms sits like an exotic desert flower in full bloom at the base of Phoenix's storied Camelback Mountain. In 1926, Delos Willard Cooke and his wife Florence came here to build their grand "winter haven," or what they called "El Vernadero."

Though wealthy New Yorkers, the Cookes felt the strong spirit of the desert. Like many who come to the Valley of the Sun for the first time, they found its allure—its aromas of citrus groves and mesquite wood smoke, the piercing blue sky and wine-streaked sunset clouds—difficult to resist. Even the great canyons of Wall Street were small and dull by comparison.

What attracted the Cookes in the 1920's, and millions of others today, is what brought the very first inhabitants to this area nearly two thousand years ago.

The Hohokam Indians were the first to settle in the

wide river basin confluence of what were later to be named the Salt and Gila Rivers. The Hohokam moved into the region in 300 B.C., traveling north from today's Mexico.

They were farmers and knew how to make water dance in the desert. They began hacking out canals from the dirt and sand with nothing more than sharpened sticks and Stone Age tools. The Hohokam carved hundreds of miles of canals, lined them with clay, fired them with brush, burned an adobe lining over them and let the river fill them with liquid nourishment.

The ribbons of water irrigated their crops of maize, beans, and squash. Living this way, the culture flourished in the warm climate for more than a millennium. Then, they vanished.

No one knows why the Hohokam left. Historians believe the climate changed and the rivers dried to dust.

An undated photo, believed to be in the late 1890's, of Camelback Mountain and the Sonoran Desert looking from the south.

CAMELBACK MT. ARIZ

Insets: (left) Aerial view of Arcadia's orange groves. (above) Phoenix founder, Jack Swilling.

Phoenix (circa 1920's) planners wanted a modern downtown, not a "sleepy Mexican village." The city was built a mile from the original town site located along the Salt River.

The Salt River Valley remained unoccupied for hundreds of years after the Hohokam. Over the centuries, a quiet parade of Spanish explorers, frontier prospectors, and military parties passed through. None saw fit to settle in this seemingly barren and hostile desert. The Pima Indians were the only ones in the valley, and they understood the magic of the place.

After the Civil War, the Arizona Territory saw the arrival of a few hardy settlers, mostly draft dodgers and war veterans prospecting for gold in nearby Wickenburg. One veteran, Jack Swilling, noticed the old Hohokam trenches stretching out like dry fingers from the Salt River. Swilling never made it to the gold mines. He was an opportunist of a different sort.

Swilling, a Confederate deserter, prospector, farmer, speculator, and opium addict, saw the United States Army establishing Camp McDowell twenty miles to the northeast. In 1865, the military's need for fresh food supplies and fodder for horses and livestock seemed insatiable. The combination of abundant land and a potentially manageable water source gave him the initiative to organize the Swilling Irrigating and Canal Company in December 1867.

He began growing hay and vegetables along the cleared out canals. His small farming enterprises attracted the attention of Englishman Darrell Dupa, who took out stock with Swilling. By 1870, the newly risen town along the river boasted a population of more than 235 and 1500 irrigated acres for farming.

Noticing that the new community was building on the old foundations of an ancient civilization, Dupa dubbed the makeshift town Phoenix—after the mythical bird that ignites in flames every five hundred years and rises again from it own ashes.

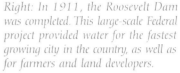

Right: In 1911, the Roosevelt Dam was completed. This large-scale Federal project provided water for the fastest growing city in the country, as well as for farmers and land developers.

Left: Reeds grow along the old Arizona Canal. It was five feet deep and fifty-eight feet wide and ran for forty miles.

Despite the objections of boosters in the city of Prescott, the growing area split off from Yavapai County. In 1871, Maricopa County was created. A Prescott native, John T. Alsap, moved to the area and became a probate judge and community leader. Soon, local boosters, speculators and hucksters began squabbling over the location of the county seat, with its guarantee of buildings, government offices, and rising real estate values.

A group, led by Swilling, pushed for an area along the river while another group promoted higher ground a mile away. That site, pressed by storekeeper James Hancock, won by sixty-two votes and backers promptly laid out a ninety-eight-block town site.

The new city grew slowly after its incorporation. Cottonwoods were planted. An ice factory and the area's first deluxe hotel were built. The town also created a canal-fed swimming pool. By 1879, the little farming community got its first railroad spur, making it possible for lumber and brick to be delivered. City leaders called for the construction of a modern "American" town, rather than a sleepy little "Mexican" village of adobe.

In 1883, the Arizona Canal project began construction of the first Valley waterway not built over the existing Hohokam canals. Two years later the Arizona Canal–which measured fifty-eight-feet wide, five-feet deep, and forty-one-miles long–opened up eighty thousand acres to cultivation.

As the farms spread, so did real estate development in the newly zoned towns of Tempe, Mesa, and Scottsdale. Area businessmen displayed an appetite for quick, relentless growth. In turn, this fueled jealousies between other nearby cities. In 1877, Prescott managed to steal the capital from Tucson, which gave schemers in Phoenix even more ideas. City backers lobbied to win the bid for the Arizona Insane Asylum, with an appropriation of $100,000.

A citrus farm at the base of Camelback Mountain near where the Royal Palms is today. Citrus is one of the four "C's" of Arizona's economy at the time. Copper, Cattle and Cotton are the other three.

Right: (above) An early advertisement aimed at easterners looking to escape cold winters. (below) With the arrival of water, the Arizona desert became a major citrus producing area.

Tucson got the leftovers— the University of Arizona, with its $25,000 appropriation. Phoenix then mounted a full-court-press to filch the capital away from Prescott, provoking newspaper columnists there to complain that "hungry, greedy Phoenix" was "selfishly reaching after the earth and the balance of the Universe."

Phoenix raised $10,000 to solicit support—a wine-and-dine fund for the legislators. A new capitol building was promised. In 1889, the town successfully convinced the legislature to remove itself from Prescott and move to Phoenix, where it remains today.

Things seemed bright until a series of disastrous floods and droughts wreaked havoc in Phoenix near the end of the century.

Realizing that construction of flood control and water storage facilities was beyond local means, state and city backers began lobbying for federal assistance. In 1904, the federal government bought a dam site. By 1911, the first reclamation project in the West was completed— Roosevelt Dam. The project provided a bounty for land speculators and farmers.

With year-round water and ideal growing conditions available, Valley farmers quickly cashed in on experimental crops of citrus and cotton. This enterprise transformed the barren desert into a paradise of palms, oranges, grapefruits and roses. Even Camelback Mountain was decked out in orange blossoms as farmers capitalized on

the abundant canal water. By 1928, more than five hundred carloads of oranges and grapefruits were shipped out of the Valley by rail each year.

Eager to capitalize on Phoenix's wide-open spaces and sunny climate, government officials started looking for new ways to promote growth. City fathers began an advertising campaign urging northerners to "winter among the palms and roses" in "Phoenix Where Summer Winters."

The tactic drew more than three thousand seasonal visitors in 1913. It was the start of what would become one of the great tourist destinations in the world—Phoenix and the Valley of the Sun.

By the late 1920's, wealthy investors from throughout the country constructed winter homes in the shadow of Camelback Mountain and in nearby Scottsdale.

The area's first residents included chewing gum magnate William Wrigley Jr., Louis Swift, Cornelius Vanderbilt, Jr., and Delos and Florence Cooke. Renowned architect Frank Lloyd Wright also fell under the spell of the Sonoran Desert. He soon began constructing his famed architectural school, Taliesin West, in 1937. In 1940, the state's bold young state senator, Barry Goldwater, declared, "the natural thing to which to turn was the capitalization of our climate, our natural beauties and the romance of our desert."

Touting Phoenix as a winter garden spot, advertising campaigns proudly proclaimed, "A person coming to the Valley of the Sun is fascinated by the thousands of acres of green and gold citrus groves; marvels at the date gardens with their graceful, swaying palms, and the soft, grey-green olive trees."

Nowhere was this more evident than in the spacious pastoral community nestled at the base of Camelback Mountain, located between Phoenix and Scottsdale.

Camelback Road was described in guidebooks as being "lined with spacious winter homes and their gardens." Particular mention was made of the Delos Cooke mansion, a Spanish Colonial Revival masterpiece on sixty-five acres of citrus trees, now home to Royal Palms Resort and Spa.

The stately historic mansion caught the public's romantic imagination with its "... long straight driveway bordered with tall palms... extraordinary specimens of greasewood and creosote bush... [and] the decorative possibilities of cultivated native plants."

By 1939, Phoenix's burgeoning tourist trade was attracting 35,000 winter visitors annually. And by the 1950's, Phoenix had seen more than a three hundred percent increase in population, making it the fastest growing city in the nation and the largest city in the Southwest.

The advent of air conditioning made the blistering summer heat more palatable. Tourism became the state's third largest source of revenue. However, Camelback Mountain began to show the strains of rapid development, which threatened to blanket the entire face of it with subdivisions. The Maricopa County Planning Commission took action in August 1956 and limited the development on the landmark to no higher than sixteen hundred feet above sea level.

The motion spurred natural resource preservation in the area. That movement provided modern day Phoenix with its abundant parks and mountain preserves. During the movement one advocate asserted, "The natural beauty of our mountain horizon, our close-in mountain slopes and natural areas—this is the very substance of the natural environment that has been so instrumental in the population and economic growth of this region. The grand scale and rugged character of these mountains have set our lifestyle, broadened our perspective, given us space to breathe, and freshened our outlook. These mountains are the plus that still overweighs the growing minuses in our environmental account."

While modern human history lies at the base of Camelback, a mass of sedimentary rock and Precambrian granite, the mountaintop remains as a staunch reminder of a longer history. Craggy trails wind up the camel's head and around its hump in a serpentine flow. Just north of the camel's head is the Grotto, an ancient place of worship. The Praying Monk, a ten-story rock monolith, serves as a reminder of the sacred mountain's link to heaven.

Seen from the summit of Camelback Mountain, Phoenix flickers with dreams and aspirations still in the making, changeable as a summer monsoon and thrilling as a coyote's cry. From this vantage point, the Praying Monk sits, silently watching the changing moods of the desert and city that rose from the ashes to bloom into a land of palms, citrus and roses.

The city of Phoenix was laid out on ninety-eight blocks. In the distance, the famous mountain that appears to be a resting camel, Camelback Mountain.

An early photograph of the famous mansion courtyard and fountain. It was designed by Lescher & Mahoney Architects to be the focal point of the Cookes' winter retreat.

*"El Vernadero was
the Cookes'
winter dream home."*

El Vernadero

*A Spanish
Colonial Dream*

It was 1926 and despite the full, heady swing of the "Jazz Age," Delos Willard Cooke at age sixty-two was tired. His career as a railroad and steamship executive in New York was coming to a close. He, a nephew of banking magnate J.P. Morgan, could now look back with pride at his long career in transportation, which included being a top executive at the Cunard Line, vice president of the Erie Railroad, and Federal Fuel Administrator for the State of New York. In addition, during the outbreak of the First World War he was responsible for transportation for the Red Cross and later was named a Chevalier of the Legion of Honor by the French Government for his services to France during the war, when he was in charge of supply movements for the Allies, and where his son, Chauncey, was fighting. The senior Cooke also received honors for his work from Italy and Great Britain.

But the winter of 1924-25 must have felt colder than most. It made Cooke think it was time to savor some of life's quieter pursuits, and to do it in warmer climes. His wife, Florence, was in ill health and had been an invalid for years. The bitter New York cold set her back to the point where Cooke knew it was time for a real change.

One day in January, while winds blustered along Wall Street, Cooke sat down at his desk and wrote his letter of resignation as associate director of the Cunard Steamship Line Company, his place of employment since The Great War.

He would retire officially on May 1, 1925, his letter stated, so he could "devote most of my time to the welfare and happiness of my wife from now on. She has first claim on me." Cooke also said that men in big business unfortunately had little time to get acquainted with their wives and family, and that this was particularly true in the transportation business.

It was not an easy decision. He was one of the company's senior executives and he would miss some of the greater advantages of position. Most of all he and his wife would miss the grand European tours via Cunard's luxury ocean liners. The winters, however, they would not miss.

They had a plan and a dream for a winter home in the great desert southwest. So, with retirement and a dream, the Cookes, along with their stockbroker son, Chauncey, began their search for their "El Vernadero," or winter haven.

Cooke read that farmers using canal water had learned to cultivate a wide variety of citrus trees and palms in central Arizona, particularly in the southern flanks of Camelback Mountain. At this time the region was producing some of Arizona's first commercial crops of navel and sweet oranges and White Marsh grapefruit.

While advertisements lured cold easterners west, the hotelier Fred Harvey and the Santa Fe Railroad teamed up to capture the imagination of even more shivering souls wishing to soak in the warm, dry climate of Arizona. They offered an easy combination of transportation and cozy hotels along the way, just the right remedy for those in fragile states of health. During the winter months, doctors actually "prescribed" prolonged stays in Arizona for their patients with respiratory ailments or arthritis.

Home developments and resorts sprouted up overnight in the former citrus groves. One new home community, called Arcadia, was created in the citrus and desert landscape along the southern edge of Camelback Mountain. It was sited halfway between Phoenix and the new desert town of Scottsdale. It was isolated country then, dusty and hot during the day, but at night a star show sparkled in the heavens. Homesites were plotted in five, twenty, and forty acres. In its early stages, Arcadia's developers had plans for a winding road to the top of Camelback with "an oasis garden" at its summit.

The road was never built, but "gentlemen farmers" from the East and Midwest found a home in Arcadia. Among them were Delos and Florence Cooke, who bought sixty-five of the best acres in an area then called Citrus Homes, which later became Arcadia. The plot, near the base of Camelback, was crowded with rows of citrus trees and had spectacular views of the ever-changing hues of the mountain, which indeed from the grounds looked like a giant, sleeping camel.

Cooke, born a Presbyterian minister's son in Lewiston, New York, was raised in the flat prairie lands of Iowa. A country boy at heart, he relished the West's wide-open spaces. The Cookes took immediately to rural Arcadia.

They arrived in the spring of 1926 and quickly sought out a top architecture firm in Phoenix to design their "El Vernadero." The couple selected the firm of Lescher & Mahoney, recognized then for its authentic Spanish Revival designs, an architectural style well suited to the desert environs and lush landscape of their property. The firm is still going strong today.

The influence of Spanish, Mediterranean, and Mexican architectural styles was enormous in Southern California and Arizona in the 1920's. Thick, whitewashed walls, colorful tiles, wrought iron fixtures and courtyard entrances were evident across the Southwest, in small tract homes to grand Hollywood estates.

Right: No aerial view exists of the original Cooke Mansion, but this photo shows the hotel in its early days. The famous heart-shaped pool is visible just to the right of the row of tall palms bordering the entrance.

Florence Cooke *Delos W. Cooke* *Chauncey Cooke*

More often than not, Spanish Revival style, a modern variation of the elegant homes found in Spain's Andalusia region, was a mix of architectural vernaculars: Spanish, Mediterranean, Spanish Colonial, Mexican Hacienda, Mission, Ranchero and California Monterey. Each variation has its own signature elements, from outdoor walkways to Arabesque influenced tiles and deep-set window openings to quiet central fountains.

Of course, the Cookes had a great time working with Lescher & Mahoney, refining plans, adding new details. Cooke's work for Cunard gave the couple access to Europe's design treasures. As a top executive with the ocean line company, they lived in Europe for a time. Their stays along the Mediterranean were still vivid memories and as blueprints developed for their winter home they added their own touches: Moorish tiles around the courtyard fountain, an original Spanish tile "mural" opposite it, iron chandeliers and wood-beamed ceilings. They also made sure there was a dramatic fireplace in the main living and entertainment area.

By June of 1926, Lescher & Mahoney completed the plans to the Cooke residence. It was a true Andalusia-inspired mansion, with flourishes of Mexico's hacienda and Spanish Colonial styles. At 3500 square feet, the home was one of the largest in Phoenix. The Cookes made sure it was sited at the end of a long, grand driveway flanked on both sides by towering palms. At a cost of one million dollars when finished, including the sixty-five acres of prime land, the Cooke's "El Vernadero" was moving rapidly from dream to reality.

It would take three years to complete the Cookes' winter retreat. It was worth the wait. In fact, much of the romantic charm found today in Royal Palms comes as much from the original detail work the Cookes incorporated into the main buildings as any other element added later.

The lush entrance to the Cooke mansion, completed in 1929.

The original "Lady of Spain" tile mural still presides over the hotel's mansion courtyard. It is believed to be one of only two that exist. The Cookes acquired the mural in Spain during one of their many trips to Europe in the 1920's.

"El Vernadero recalls some of Mexico's finest Spanish and French Colonial influences."

A true Spanish Colonial-inspired design with Mediterranean and hacienda flourishes, the Cooke home stood apart from the other homes hidden in the shadow of Camelback Mountain and shade of citrus groves. For privacy, Cooke immediately constructed a two-mile-long, seven-foot-high stone and white adobe wall around the property. Legend has it that Cooke spent seventy thousand dollars to construct the fence alone.

The entrance to "El Vernadero" was from the south, through an oversized pair of ancient wooden gate doors that opened to a zaguan, or covered breezeway. On either side of the driveway, Florence Cooke installed elegant tall runs of palms.

Lescher & Mahoney's plan from the start was to have the home centered on a central courtyard and fountain, in the manner of Spain's grand Andalusian estates in the hills north of Marbella. It also recalled some of Mexico's finest Spanish and French Colonial influences, particularly in intricate iron and tile work. The home was designed to have white plaster over brick walls, Granada-tiled roofs, grillwork for windows and doors, and smoothly rounded arches throughout. It was a style very much in vogue.

The core of the Cookes' home centered on the courtyard and its lushly landscaped, Moorish-influenced, reflecting pool. The architects wrapped the home around this central water feature. In keeping with the Spanish Colonial tradition and the warm climate, the design also called for no interior hallways, but rather arched arcades. These shady outdoor portales along the courtyard's perimeter led guests from one end of the house to the other. The only exceptions were hallways connecting the owner's private bedrooms.

The home's living room was located at the front of the structure. Today it is called "Vernadero Room" and is set up for private dinners and meetings. It is set apart from other rooms by its formal gloss, high-beamed ceiling and dramatic fireplace. The main guest room at the front of the structure is the current check-in lobby for the hotel. The long west wing line of rooms, then just one story, contained the Cookes' complex of bedrooms, dressing rooms and bathrooms.

The original north wing of the home was where the Cookes entertained. The main function rooms, dining, billiards, and kitchen were all housed in this large rectangular section. All the rooms had views of the citrus groves, the mountain or the graceful courtyard fountain.

The architects also included many smaller rooms behind the north wing. These rooms were for servants, a chauffer, storage and small kitchen for workers, a tool room, and large garage.

While the Cookes watched their winter home rise among the groves, they began seeking out new and old treasures for the interior and outside living areas. Many pieces they found on their European travels when Cooke worked for

"One need only to look at the details to see that this mansion was a masterpiece."

Cunard. They were inveterate antique collectors. Many of their priceless, fifteenth century antique pieces from Spain and Italy would soon find a new home in Phoenix.

There are dozens of original "Cooke features" that still exist at Royal Palms today. The authentic central courtyard design element is still the focal point of the property. This "quiet area" provides visitors with a sense of discovery. New courtyards were added over the years, using original outdoor fireplaces and antique fountains. Like everything about the property, the key idea of gracious desert living was to "stop and pause."

The most enduring tribute to the home is the imported Spanish tile mural of "The Lady of Spain" that enjoys the same placement on the courtyard wall since the day it was placed there by the Cookes. Looking out on the courtyard, "The Lady," in all her brightly glazed elegance, welcomes everyone who enters the courtyard and T. Cook's Restaurant.

The heavy wooden doors at the front and side entrances to Royal Palms are the original mahogany doors the Cookes installed when they built the home. The courtyard reflecting pool still retains its original Moorish shape, but new hand-painted tiles from Portugal were added during restoration work. Visitors today can see twenty-four original tiles imbedded in the courtyard walls. These crest tiles represent the provinces of Spain.

The Cookes were devout Catholics and on a side wall near their bedrooms they installed an an ivory-colored bas-relief wall sculpture of Christ. Evidence of their strong faith can be seen in a crest above the main entrance on the east side of the structure. It reads: *En Dieu Est Ma Fiance* or "To God I Am Betrothed."

Most of the wrought iron work on the windows and doorways is original, too. Other iron pieces, like sconces and railings, were copied later during the property's restoration to match originals found in old photographs.

Once the home was sited and construction began, Florence Cooke began the large task of landscaping the property into her vision of a desert-bound Mediterranean villa. Her husband granted her an annual landscaping allowance of ten thousand dollars for the property. In the end, El Vernadero ended up with over nine hundred palms, many rare, as well as the existing citrus trees, exotic flowers and shrubs, and numerous specimen cacti.

Today, the property sits on nine acres, but many of Florence Cooke's original palms can be found, including such varieties as Mexican fan, California fan, Mediterranean fan, pindo, sago, Canary Island, date, sabal, windmill fan, Pigmy date and, of course, Royal.

The courtyard garden alone boasted some fifty species of plants, including jasmines, palms, coral trees, lemon trees, birds of paradise, cape honeysuckle, thevetia, sable, windmill palms, and bougainvillea.

Now, the courtyard garden remains one of the most serene places on the property and a good place to take in both the old and new romance of Royal Palms.

A wrought-iron gate leads to one of the hotel's quiet pathways and "discovery areas." The hotel is noted for its many original tile and wrought-iron features throughout the property.

THE DEFINITION OF STYLES

Architects who specialize in authentic Southwestern and Spanish Revival design often have a difficult time defining the style they are creating: Is it Mexican Hacienda, Territorial, Spanish Colonial, Ranchero, Monterey-style, or Mediterranean? To the untrained eye the subtleties may seem small, but to aficionados of the many types of Southwestern architecture the differences are easy to spot and appreciate. Like many dwellings built in the 1920's, the heyday of Spanish Colonial and Mediterranean building period, the Cooke home (today's Royal Palms), was a well-designed hybrid of Spanish Colonial, Mexican Hacienda, and Mediterranean styles.

Right: Iron nailheads, or clavos, on a doorway.

Below: The graceful arches of the central courtyard.

Left: The angelic cherub placed in the center of the Moorish-influenced fountain in the mansion courtyard.

Spanish Colonial

This style of design is noted for its interior patio and fountain with decorative wrought-iron work, Moorish tiles and heavy moldings around doors and windows. Homes of this style generally have more embellished European and French accents. These come from France's colonization of Mexico—hence the term Spanish Colonial. The colonial style often reflects both French and Spanish designs. It also uses stronger colors, especially yellow, rose, and green, that have been popular in Mexico for centuries.

Mediterranean

The Mediterranean style is inspired by the earthy, bold, contrasting colors of the countries surrounding the Mediterranean Sea. These include the rich reds and blues, dazzling white lime-wash, yellows, and earthy terracotta hues. The Mediterranean is the crossroads of design, texture and color–the melting pot of East and West, Africa and Asia. Textile and tile designs often use Arabic patterns. Doorways and windows use Moorish arches. Courtyard fountains also have traditional Moorish/Arabesque flairs. Wrought-iron window grills and balconies are common design elements. These often make for colorful display areas for geraniums, daisies and other fragrant plants that contrast nicely with white-washed doors and faded-blue shutters.

Left (top and bottom): Painted scroll-like palms offer up images of the Mediterranean, while tile work shows French inspiration.

Right: The domed entry ceiling and intricate iron chandelier are typically Spanish and Mexican in style.

Mexican Hacienda

This is the true Mexican style of architecture. Its heritage dates from before the colonization of Mexico by the Spanish and French. In later years, the big working haciendas were greatly influenced by Moorish, Spanish, and European design elements. This style relies heavily on the use of natural stone, adobe, wood, cantera stone, and red tile roofs. It is a very simple style. It often incorporates brick domes in central greeting areas, cantera stone floors and marble or saltillo flooring. Colors go with basic tones of the earth. A key feature is that the home is built around an interior patio and the main doorway leads directly to it. The functional purpose for this design was that the home's water came from a well in the middle of a central patio. The thick walls provided security. It is considered a very practical design style for the climate and lifestyle of Mexico in the early and late 1800's.

Over the years, Royal Palms has incorporated many styles, including Spanish Colonial, Mediterranean, and Mexican Hacienda. Rustic, but decorative wooden door headers are typical of rural Mexico, while elaborate Spanish candleholders fit nicely with elegant and formal interiors. The tile design in the resort's central courtyard fountain is inspired by Moorish patterns found throughout the Mediterranean region.

The Royal Palms Inn as it looked in the 1950's. The original Cooke Mansion was only one story. The second story and tower were added by the home's second owner, W.E. Travis, president of Greyhound Bus Lines. The low buildings on the left were guest suites added in the late 1940's by Al Stovall, the bandleader who turned the grand mansion into a hotel.

The Royal Palms Is Born

"The naming of
the Inn
was obvious...
All one had to do
was look at
the stately palms
flanking the
grand drive
off Camelback Road."

For two years Delos and Florence Cooke enjoyed their new home in Arcadia until his death at the age of 66. Intestinal cancer had taken its toll and a recent operation, and its complications, took a man that "was beloved by thousands," according to automobile magnate Walter P. Chrysler, a close friend.

Shaken by the sudden death of her husband in 1931, Florence Cooke continued wintering at the estate, working on her gardens, and maintaining their dream. But six years later, and failing in health again, Florence Cooke sold the mansion and its grounds to W.E. Travis, then president of Greyhound Bus Lines.

The wealthy Travis and his family settled into their new Arizona home with great appreciation for what the Cookes had accomplished. Travis and his wife made great efforts to keep the home true to the original dream, but they did make several major improvements. The greatest change was the addition of a second story over the west wing. This addition was used as their private quarters.

As part of the second floor expansion, Travis, like the Cookes, also seemed a highly religious man and added a small chapel to the religious elements already in place. The Travis family settled into the home for more than five years, but in 1942 Travis' wife passed away. The estate, now too big to manage alone, was sold to the president of the Aviola Radio Company, John Ross.

Ross quickly sold half the property, some thirty-five acres, to home developers. He held onto the rest of the estate for six years and then, for unknown reasons, sold the remaining thirty acres and the mansion to a group of investors led by former bandleader Al Stovall.

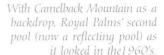

With Camelback Mountain as a backdrop, Royal Palms' second pool (now a reflecting pool) as it looked in the 1960's.

The year was 1948 and Stovall, who made a fortune in manganese and copper mining, foresaw a boom in Arizona tourism after the war. He looked at the old Cooke mansion and its surrounding lush landscape as an ideal property for a winter retreat and inn for his well-to-do business friends and Hollywood celebrities.

Stovall went about convincing his partners, which included Fred Dreier as principal and president of the new Royal Palms Operating Company Inc., to build fifteen hotel rooms to the west of the original Cooke home. He also planned to take the main house and convert its rooms into a charming complex of guest rooms, entertainment areas, lounges, reception, and dining rooms. Under Stovall's hand, the inn's amenities included new tennis courts, horseback riding, and a fanciful heart-shaped swimming pool with antique delft tiles.

Of course, the naming of the inn was obvious. All one had to do was look at the stately palms flanking the grand drive leading off Camelback Road and into the estate. They were the same palms Florence Cooke installed twenty years earlier.

With these changes completed, Al Stovall's Royal Palms Inn opened to its first guests in the winter of 1948. Officially, Royal Palms opened on the first of February, 1948. A night's stay was thirty-five dollars.

Over the next four years, Stovall built another forty-five guest "casitas." These were located on the east side of the property. Before too long, Royal Palms became one of the "in places" to stay during the winter season.

Though Stovall and Dreier had a good run with the inn, the investment group decided to sell the property in late 1951 to businessman Barney Leonard, for less than $125,000.

Leonard knew a wise investment when he saw it. Thankfully, he changed little about the property, but after four years he too decided to sell. The inn was sold (for $500,000) to a six-person syndicate of midwestern investors headed by Fred W. Renker, a former nationally ranked tennis player and one-time manager of the nearby Paradise Inn. Having managed many hotels and clubs, Renker knew the potential of Royal Palms. In no time, he raised the money and in 1956 he and his partners were the new owners. Each member of the syndicate put in $50,000 and the remaining $200,000 was a bank loan.

Renker ushered in the most glamorous era for Royal Palms. He hosted dozens of celebrities each season and understood how to cater to their quirky demands. But by 1961, Renker and his partners said it was time to cash in their investment. They sold Royal Palms to Chicago investor and hotelier, Charles Alberding, who sat down one day with Renker and said: "I think I'd like to buy your hotel." To this day, Renker said selling it was the "worst decision of my life."

Alberding owned the Texas-based company Alsonett Hotels. The company owned and managed a chain of hotels from Florida to California. Some of its more famous properties were The Peabody Hotel in Memphis and The Torrey Pines Inn in San Diego. As part of the chain, Alberding also owned and managed two nearby and popular Camelback Mountain area resorts: The Jokake Inn and The Paradise Inn (which Renker managed in 1953). But Alberding, a savvy hotel man, saw his newest acquisition as his "jewel in the desert."

Alberding set about immediately to transition Royal Palms into an elegant boutique inn that would compete with the finest resorts in the rapidly growing Phoenix market.

While living in Chicago, Alberding personally oversaw the hotel's improvements, including new meeting rooms, a new kitchen, expansion of the dining room, a new lobby and reception area, and a modern pool. In 1981, Alberding additions included building a two-story structure with underground parking and sixty-eight additional guest suites. He even installed a regulation, par 36, nine-hole golf course on the remaining acreage.

The new owner filled his jewel with fine oil paintings, crystal chandeliers, and oriental rugs. Alberding had the longest stewardship of the property up until that time. Unfortunately, in the early 1970's, a fire broke out and destroyed a large section of the hotel. To manage its rebuilding and management, Alberding installed his long-time personal secretary, Pat Ryan, as overseer.

Ryan, who lived in Chicago at the time, started in 1972 as general manager of the hotel and planned to spend a year re-organizing and bringing the inn back to its prior glory. She stayed for twenty-two years.

Ryan became a legend and was known as one of Phoenix's most gracious innkeepers, a tough task among the good 'ole boys that ran the hotel business then. Her dogs were always lounging about near guests or on the lobby sofa. Among regulars, the dogs affectionately became known as the manager's four-legged desk clerks.

In the late 1970's, Ryan managed the inn well enough to keep it going in the hot summer months. Her lure was

music. In the 1980's, she was one of the first hoteliers to start booking small orchestras and singers. She set up a small stage and dance floor in the Orange Tree Dining Room and outside patio areas. The inn soon became the place to go in Phoenix for a romantic night of dancing and music under the palms. By the late 1980's, Ryan was attracting such stars as Tony Martin, Frank Sinatra, Jr., Patty Andrews (of the Andrews Sisters) and Sandler and Young. Well-known business leaders, like Malcolm Baldridge and Neil "Moon" Reagan (Ronald's brother) were regulars, preferring Ryan's and Royal Palms' personal style to some of the larger area resorts. Ryan was able to snare one of the most well-known restauranteurs in the Valley, Louis Germaine, to run her food department. Germaine owned the well-known Chez Louis in the 1950's and when he decided to sell it he accepted Ryan's offer to run the Orange Tree.

In 1989, Ryan's visionary boss, Charles Alberding, died at the age of eighty-eight. It was the end of an era. The Alberding reign lasted almost thirty years.

In 1995, the Alberding family began thinking about selling the property and the inn. Later that year they sold the golf course to Doug Sandahl of Montecito Homes. Sandahl later developed twenty-nine single-family homes. Not long after selling the land, the family then sold the inn to Fred and Jennifer Unger.

The Ungers were local hoteliers. They had just completed the restoration of the historic The Hermosa Inn in nearby

Left: Hotel owner/manager Fred Renker (right) with friend and partner Felix Havemann.

Right: The famous heartshaped pool and what is now called the Vernadero Lawn. The pool and tennis court were later removed during the restoration in the late 1990's.

Paradise Valley. The Hermosa Inn was once the home and studio of Arizona's legendary cowboy artist, Lon Megargee.

Fred Unger thought there was tremendous potential. He turned to his wife's old family friend, Cecil Van Tuyl, the wealthy car dealer and real estate investor from Kansas City.

As the design team began, the process of the original scope was quickly seen to be unrealistic. There was a need for new mechanical systems (a cost of four to five million dollars alone), kitchen, and banquet facilities. The target was raised from a simple, conservative remodel to one of a complete nine-acre restoration.

"Cecil was a modest man," Unger says. "He had a hard time believing people would spend $350 a night for a hotel room. It got a little intense as the costs mounted. For us, it was damned the torpedoes. It had to be one hundred percent or it was a waste. We'd save money with plastic ashtrays, but it would ruin the effect we were after, a private home."

If nothing else, their experience at The Hermosa Inn taught them one very important lesson: successful resorts of this size must be food driven. From the very start, they knew the restaurant, the newly named T. Cook's, had to stand on its own.

"The moment a customer walks into the courtyard of Royal Palms they've bought into the idea of great food," Jennifer Unger says. "We had to follow through on that expectation."

T. Cook's excellent reputation would give the hotel a strong point of differentiation, the key ingredient in the property's strategy for success.

To the Ungers, Royal Palms was a work of art and as a year of intense restoration ensued, the costs quickly escalated as the scope changed from a three-star to a five-star resort. In the end, it cost the Ungers and their sole backer, Van Tuyl, almost $28 million, and sadly their ownership in the hotel.

Above: A section of the Orange Tree Dining Room, now T. Cook's. Right: Fred Renker (center) and his staff preparing for a Sunday buffet.

Nevertheless, the Ungers employed some unusual methods in the restoration. The goal was to upgrade and restore the property to its original grandeur of the late 1920's and 30's. But they wanted its romantic nature amplified into a style that fit with the tastes of the modern, seasoned travelers seeking unique, high-end accommodations.

To accomplish this they had to close the property entirely, begin work immediately, including removing the inn's beloved heart-shaped pool.

The year of the restoration was 1996 and the Ungers were able to persuade the local chapter of the American Society of Interior Design to use the entire Royal Palms as their fundraising "Showcase Home." It was quite a coup. It was the first time the ASID agreed to design the renovation of a commercial property. Over twenty

separate design teams participated. The theme the Ungers asked the designers to use was "Spanish Colonial-Mediterranean." However, the influences of the desert Southwest and Mexico were not to be denied. This style was also fittingly incorporated into the showcase by several teams. Today, these rooms are now called the "Designer Casitas."

The Ungers knew food was the key to success and so the old Orange Tree Dining Room was renamed T. Cook's (mistakenly in honor of the long-dying myth that Delos Cooke was travel legend Thomas Cook). Jim Smith, hotel and restaurant consultant, came up with the idea of an elegant, Mediterranean-themed restaurant centered on a

fireplace that was then hidden by stacks of dining room chairs.

The plan was to build a "buzz" among locals for great food and service, along with old world charm, while the restoration was underway. T. Cook's would add to the anticipation of the grand "re-opening." It was only realized later that banker/steamship executive Cooke was not the travel king Cook, but they stuck with the myth anyway. "It became part of the legend of the restaurant," Smith said, recalling those early days. With or without the legend, T. Cook's menu of rustic Mediterranean fare became an instant classic.

Today, Royal Palms Resort and Spa, and T. Cook's, is recognized internationally with prestigious awards from such acclaimed publications as *Conde Nast Traveler*, *Travel + Leisure*, *The Robb Report*, and *Andrew Harper's Hideaway*. But in 1997, few knew what was to come.

In April of 1997, the "new" Royal Palms opened for business and the first guests arrived. Even without awards, Ungers' masterpiece caught the eye of Destination Hotels & Resorts, a subsidiary of Lowe Enterprises, and it soon became part of its portfolio of properties. Royal Palms is now one of the company's over thirty independent, upscale and luxury hotels, resorts, and golf clubs in the United States. Since its restoration, Royal Palms has continued to improve, with the addition of the Alvadora Spa and the new Montavista Collection of suites and rooms, bringing the resort's room total to 119.

*"Hollywood's biggest
stars called the
Royal Palms home."*

The Golden Era

It was the beginning of yet another new era for the great hotel. Hollywood and Royal Palms were linked together from the first day the old Delos Cooke mansion was converted to an inn in 1948.

The match was an instant success. Al Stovall, a former bandleader and manganese millionaire, bought the sixty-five acre property with an eye for creating a desert watering hole, an oasis for his high-rolling business and celebrity friends. He brought in a group of like-minded investors and began the conversion from home to hotel. He immediately put the word out: Royal Palms Inn, the "Jewel of Phoenix," was open for business.

The first celebrities to arrive during "the season" – January through April – were New Yorkers Helena Rubenstein, the cosmetics empire founder, and comic film star Groucho Marx. With accolades from these two celebrities, word spread quickly, and soon Royal Palms became the center of Arizona's Hollywood elite.

In the 1940's and 50's, Phoenix was known as having a strong regional theater market. This was decades before the explosive growth of Las Vegas and the California desert resort scene. The area's most famous theater was The Sombrero Playhouse on Seventh Street and Camelback Road, a short trip from the hotel.

The list of Hollywood and New York luminaries that walked the boards at The Sombrero and stayed at Royal Palms is long and illustrious: Vincent Price, Robert Ryan, the Gabor sisters, the Gish sisters, Joan Blondell, Joan Bennett, Buster Keaton, Edwin Everett Horton, Jack Elam, Brian Donlevy, and Walter Pidgeon, are but a few. Fred Renker, owner and general manager in the late 1950's, made the hotel a sanctuary and often put their names on the inn's large Camelback Road sign.

Above: Local theater brought out the stars to the Royal Palms. A Royal Palms regular, actress Eva Gabor, caught by photographers outside the front entrance with her ever present "Baby," a Yorkshire terrier.

Left: Actor Vincent Price, his wife, the hotel's chef and former owner and operator Fred Dreier.

Bandleader Vaughn Monroe with his helicopter pilot John Holefelder.

The Gish sisters.

Edward Everett Horton reading script with fellow actor (unnamed).

Often, Eva Gabor swept into the lobby wearing her mink and with her Yorkshire terrier, "Baby," clutched under her arm. The Gabor sisters lived up to their reputations as demanding and theatrical, on stage and off. One year, Eva settled into her suite for several months while appearing in the play "Blithe Spirit" and was often spotted swimming naked in the heart-shaped pool.

Renker and his wife, Sarah, had a special talent for hosting Hollywood's biggest players. Renker, a seasoned hotelier and accomplished tennis professional, said he often saw Buster Keaton and Walter Pidgeon sunning poolside. Pidgeon was usually reading a new movie script or relaxing under a palo verde tree with his agent.

Stage and film star Edward Everett Horton enjoyed his stays so much, and was such a steady visitor, he knew every staff member by first name.

Three-time Oscar winner Charlie Coburn was famous around the inn not only for his signature monocle, but also for his antics. Coburn, a ribald man of eighty years in 1958, was usually spotted dancing late into the evenings, drinking and smoking cigars. He was known for his marathon poker playing sessions, some lasting fifteen hours at a stretch.

Billionaire Howard Hughes was a secretive player throughout his life, but when it came to one of his longest loves, a vivacious starlet named Terry Moore, his stealth operatives went into high gear to protect their privacy. Hughes often took over entire sections of hotels. The two would never emerge. With or without Hughes, Moore was often spotted at the inn, secluded in her own casita, only to come out for a short swim.

From its earliest days, Royal Palms was known as a dinner and dancing nightspot. During "the season," big name orchestras serenaded guests under the desert stars.

Orchestra leader Vaughan Monroe arrived by private helicopter for his tours in Phoenix. He landed his rotor aircraft directly on the hotel's front drive, stirring up dust and a lot of excitement with his arrival. One arrival ended abruptly when a wind gust tossed the helicopter

Right: Oscar-winner, monocle-wearing Charles Coburn poses with hotel guests (left) Mill McWirther and Luella Koford, mother of actress Terry Moore.

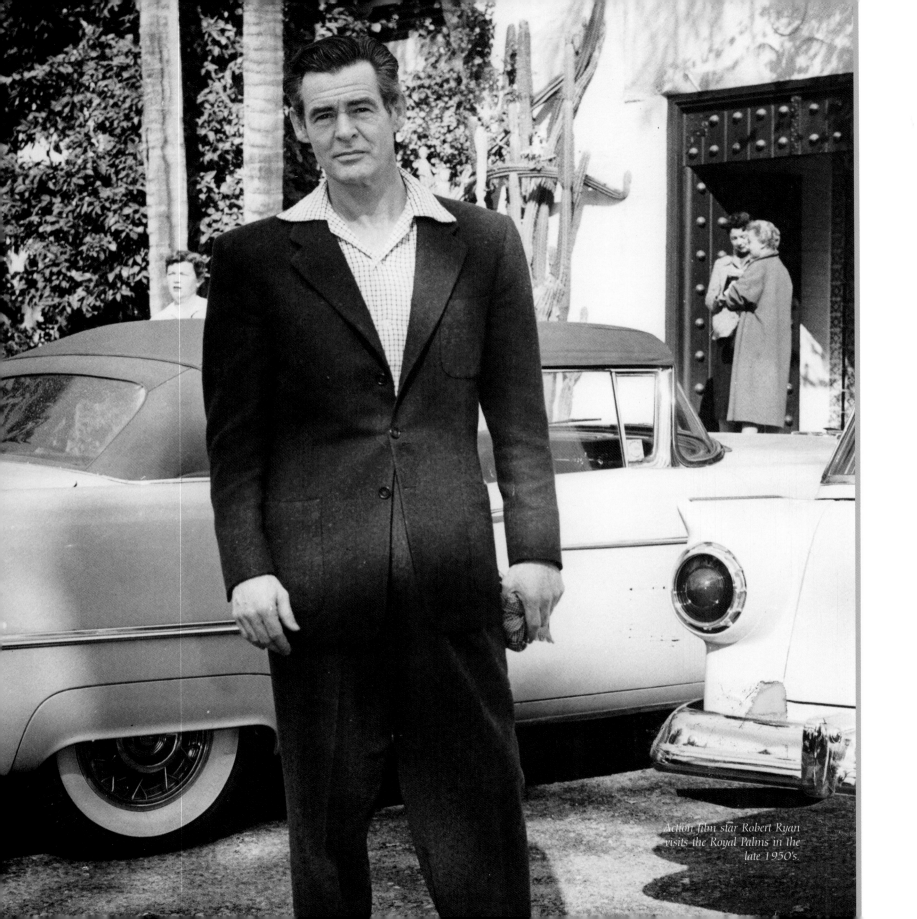

Action film star Robert Ryan visits the Royal Palms in the late 1950's.

Actress Terry Moore and mother, Luella Koford. Moore is known as the legal widow of billionaire Howard Hughes.

Comic genius Buster Keaton.

Funnyman Wally Cox.

into the top of a palm just behind the hotel. Fortunately, everyone walked away.

In the 1960's, ownership of the hotel changed to Chicagoan Charles Alberding and his manager then, Pat Ryan, began booking small orchestras and singers for the then named Orange Tree Dining Room.

Ryan ushered in a new golden era for the property. Every Saturday night, well-known singers, bands and musical performers were fixtures at Royal Palms. Phoenix area residents and guests alike came to hear such regulars as Tony Martin, Frank Sinatra, Jr., Patty Andrews, Sandler and Young and local stars, The Hallmans. Frankie Carle, composer of Sunrise Serenade, was a frequent diner at the Orange Tree.

In 1993, music producer Bob Lorenz created a series of summer jazz nights. Lorenz brought in many of the era's greatest jazz horn players, percussionists, and pianists to

Walter Pidgeon (right) sits pool-side talking Hollywood business with hotel guest.

play for the crowds. Many of the players were former members of the Stan Kenton Band, and the Monday, Tuesday, and Wednesday swings became known as the Kenton Alumni Series.

Singer and guitarist Glen Campbell was a neighbor and when he was married many of his guests stayed at the inn. On his fiftieth birthday, his wife took over the Orange Tree dining room for a surprise party.

The property has been featured on the big screen. In 1991, the movie Sunstroke, starring Jane Seymour and Don Ameche, was filmed throughout the property.

Couples danced under palms and starry nights. Twinkling white lights cast a romantic spell. The sweet mixture of the desert's unique aromas, citrus blossoms and mesquite smoke, filled the air. This legacy of romance continues to this day.

Today, Royal Palms reflects the essence of a grand Mediterranean residence where guests feel at home. The centuries-old fountain and hand-cut stone pavers were acquired from a Mexican village's central plaza.

"The new Royal Palms was to reflect the grace and style of a bygone era. The resort was meant to feel like a rich uncle's estate."

The New Royal Palms

The re-birth of the "new" Royal Palms was not an easy delivery, and to this day it continues to be improved, added to, and enhanced. Most recently, the hotel has seen the additions of the Montavista Collection of rooms and suites and the world-class Alvadora Spa.

But back in late 1995, Royal Palms was a jewel in bad need of repair, re-setting, and a lot of polish to get it to the right level of luster necessary to attract patrons seeking luxury accommodations. In fact, the property was just days away from being bulldozed for a single-family home development.

The tower on the property's
northwest corner leads to the
Priest's Suite.

Left: One of the many arches and wrought-iron gates of Royal Palms.

Right: An antique rustic table beneath a gated window adds to the resort's residential ambiance.

The old Cooke mansion and its surrounding casitas were in dire need of new plumbing and electrical systems, updated meeting rooms, and nearly all of the guest suites needed complete makeovers. In addition, there was a need for the construction of new luxury villas, commercial kitchen, and new pool. Though it was not the original goal, Royal Palms would soon turn into the area's next luxury resort. In the end, the vision would be realized, but the cost was high–close to $28 million.

From the beginning, the concept for the restoration was to go back to the original feel and ambiance of the Cookes' Spanish Colonial mansion and not create the feeling of a hotel.

One great advantage was that "charm" in Phoenix was in short supply. The new Royal Palms was to reflect the grace and style of a bygone era, according to Fred Unger, the new owner, at the time. The resort was meant to "feel like a rich uncle's estate."

To assist in the restoration was Jim Smith, of Serving the Nation, an upscale hospitality and concept consulting firm. Smith spent time walking the grounds and came up with the initial overview concept for an upscale, romantic, residential-themed property. A number of architects were interviewed, but eventually selected a new arrival to Phoenix, Don Ziebell, of OZ Architects, to work closely with them to insure the creation of their desired vision.

Ziebell knew the old property well. He had played the old nine-hole executive course a number of times and, for him, the mansion was an intriguing architectural challenge, since most hotel companies at the time were looking to build modern, mega-sized southwestern resorts. The idea of a small, Old World-style resort was a fresh notion for the market.

Encouraged by this vision for the property, the new owners went about raising the capital to make Royal Palms a reality. Unger made one call to an old family friend, Cecil

A casita's private patio.

The residence's original owners, the Cookes, were extremely religious. Just off the central courtyard they installed this bas-relief bust of Christ that is still there today.

A striking earthenware artifact stands just off the mansion courtyard.

Van Tuyl, one the largest auto dealers in the country. After buying the property for three and a half million, Van Tuyl agreed to another six to seven million for improvements to get the hotel up to modern standards as a quaint, luxury inn. But getting it to that level, took considerably more.

General contractors Hardison/Downey were hired to manage the project. The builders were told that the restoration schedule, from start to finish, would be nine months. Then, Smith contacted interior designer Joszi Meskan from San Francisco, whom he had collaborated with on other projects like the Hotel Del Coronado, to get her advice on the interior moods. There were two landscape designers: Peter Crue of Arterra and Greg Trutza of New Directions in Landscape Architecture. To round out the restoration team, Randy Brown, operations vice president in Unger's office, suggested to Smith and Ziebell that Georgia Bates, a Mexican architectural antiques specialist, be brought in to help source antique building materials. A few months later, Unger and Brown found and hired Greg Miller away from Hyatt Hotels to manage the property.

Royal Palms' owners wanted a team builder and someone who could open a hotel under the pressure of construction. Miller had just that experience. Beginning his career with Pan American Airways in New York in 1980, Miller switched over to the hotel side of the travel business and joined the Hyatt organization. His first assignment was at New York's Grand Hyatt after the massive renovation of the old Commodore Hotel. For the next 15 years he opened the Hyatt Regency Grand Cypress in Orlando, Hyatt Westshore in Tampa, and Hyatt Regency Grand Cayman. After an assignment at the new, local Hyatt Regency Scottsdale, he found himself on his next big mission—the Grand

The furnishings throughout the property reflect the desire to make it feel like an elegant residence.

Just off the Presidential and Honeymoon Villas, a circular fountain and grass area delight the eyes and ears of visitors.

Hyatt Wailea, Maui. This $600 million property was billed by its owners as the greatest resort in the world and served as the flagship resort for Hyatt. After three years at the Hyatt Regency Waikiki, Unger lured Miller from Hawaii.

"It was a leap of faith to leave Hyatt, but it turned out to be a great career move," Miller says. "I knew the possibilities for Royal Palms were enormous and it was a great opportunity to step out from under the corporate umbrella and apply my years of experience to an extraordinary hotel project with unlimited potential."

Miller arrived at Royal Palms in July, 1996, just as the heavy construction and demolition were beginning. He went to work immediately creating a team, planning food service, building supplier relationships, implementing marketing plans, and "polishing this stone into a gem."

But the full scope of the restoration was still not clearly understood. Miller looked around at open trenches, the demolition, and at the workmen sweating in the summer heat. The task looked impossible. "But everyone was determined to complete it one way or another."

To add to the construction complexity, the hotel had booked weddings and social events well in advance, thinking that the property would be ready in time. To handle this additional tumult, the team erected a tented, triage-style kitchen to handle the numerous upcoming events. Two other massive tents were added to serve as ballrooms until the restored salons were ready. The tents stood for five months.

Even then the food and service were exceptional, according to Miller. And guests were more than understanding. "They began to feel like they were playing a role in our history, it was great to be a part of it," he says

looking back now. He admits there were many heroes who embraced these operational challenges and did whatever it took to get results. It was the start of a transformation unlike any other seen in the hospitality industry.

Before the restoration work began, the first thing the team did was reconnaissance: a quick two-day trip to hotels from San Diego to Napa Valley. This provided ideas and a feel for what they were after. For example, the small, charming Bel-Air Hotel, nestled in the hills of Bel-Air Estates in Los Angeles, was one the team particularly admired. They liked its low-rise nature, its lawns and its feeling of arriving at a luxurious villa—and they liked the oval-shaped swimming pool, which the current pool was eventually modeled after.

When it came to understanding the kind of furnishings the hotel would require, they leaned on Meskan, while Bates' mission was to supply the restorers with an almost endless stream of stone pieces, wrought-iron fixtures, carved-wood furniture, antique doors, wood beams and pavers.

In search of authenticity, the team of Unger, Ziebell, and Bates went on an antique-hunting trip to Mexico. The first stop was to Guadalajara, to buy old wood doors with hand-forged iron details. There, they found a rare, two-hundred-and-fifty-year-old yellow cantera stone fountain. This was earmarked immediately for the hotel's front entrance. Additional cities were visited for cantera stone tiles for the swimming pool. From a ruined hacienda in Querretero they found ancient laja negra (black stone) and laja rosa (red stone) pavers. And many of the antiques and ceramic tiles were purchased in the beautiful colonial city of Puebla.

On the same trip, Ziebell noticed an old town street being torn up. The four-hundred-year-old pavers were being tossed to make way for asphalt. Ziebell cut a deal on the spot to have the stones shipped north. The stones were over six inches thick and dated from 1692 (an inscription on one stone has the date carved into it). These blocks now grace the hotel's front entrance.

The trips to Mexico proved invaluable. It gave them a keener, deeper appreciation of the history and culture behind the things they sought and wanted to infuse into Royal Palms. Even before Unger purchased the resort, Smith's strongest vision was to reposition the entrance and reception areas of the hotel back to the mansion's south entrance and then use the mansion to set the character for the entire project. Over the years, they discovered, parts of the old house were requisitioned for any number of uses that served its many owners. Some rooms were used for offices and others were used for employee dining. The reception, which over the years had floated from one location to another (at one time was located near the current entrance of T. Cook's and prior to the restoration was placed near the current Cervantes Lounge), was moved to the front of the property, the Cookes' original front guest room.

The original living room was turned into a lavish boardroom-style meeting room or formal dining room, now called "Vernadero". He also re-positioned the entrance to the old Orange Tree Dining Room back inside the mansion, at the end of the arched and columned walkway that passes the Moorish-style reflecting pool. The T. Cook's name change came in the fall, but already the transformation was underway.

Vernadero is a royal venue for a one-of-a-kind dining or meeting experience. The fireplace and impressive wood ceiling are all original. It was the Cooke family's formal living room in the late 1920's.

This intimate seating area is located just off the Lounge. The cozy room has a unique leather floor, deep set sofas and provides an ideal setting for private conversations.

Next, Ziebell put his drafting pencil to the 1950's-era additions on the property's eastern side. After several existing structures were razed, he oversaw their replacements, one housing a gracious ballroom and the other a series of meeting rooms. All of the hotel's casitas were to be completely gutted and expanded with private patios. Pleasant, meandering walkways were also created with outdoor sitting areas, fireplaces and gurgling fountains. These were looked at as points of inspiration, or discovery spaces, as guests made their way from their rooms to the interior of the property. Ziebell's new plan also called for the building of four new, luxury villas. The old two-story Plaza building, now the newly re-designed Montavista, also received a Spanish Colonial facelift in 1997. And that section would receive an even greater renovation a decade later.

The loss of the famed heart-shaped pool, and the legendary Cantina Bar, was a true heartbreaker for those who loved the old Royal Palms. The new owners took a lot of heat for filling in and knocking down these pieces of local lore, but the pool leaked horribly (hundreds of gallons a day) and the new size of the hotel required additional parking, by code. Something had to be sacrificed. In addition, Smith's vision called for a classic, carriage entrance architectural statement for arriving guests. The old pool was located in the only reasonable area where additional parking could be accommodated.

A larger, oval-shaped pool was built on the eastern side of the property, directly in front of what is now the Montavista. The old rectangular pool was turned into a long reflecting pool flanked on one side by an emerald green lawn and cozy outdoor sitting areas.

What the team liked about the project was that they could be hands-on with the project from the beginning to end, even if the restoration schedule was daunting, perhaps even naïve.

The original time frame Unger laid out to the architect was to start work in January of 1996 and finish everything by the start of the next tourist season in October. The team laughs at this notion now.

"The time frame was crazy, but in a way it helped us," Ziebell says, in recalling those days. "We didn't belabor design decisions and we just pointed and yelled a lot at the construction crews. If it looked reasonable it was a go. We lived and worked this way at the site for a year." He refers to the entire restoration process as "blow and go. Demolition and design on the fly. Permitting as needed."

There were a total of fourteen separate permits. The City of Phoenix stood by the project from beginning to end, cooperating and issuing permits as things needed changing.

The west side casitas were first to be ripped apart. He created the Spanish sense of enclosure by adding fountains, curving walkways, walls, and outdoor fireplaces. Ziebell managed the process and also sourced much of the antique building material for the project. This included heavy gauge, decorative iron brackets to hold ceiling timbers (one hundred-year-old rail trestle pulled from The Great Salt Lake) and ancient pavers from dusty towns in Mexico, to name just a few of the hundreds of specialty items needed to create the classic residential effect the team sought.

Craftsmen in Mexico were located to create the unique round bricks used for columns found throughout the property. A local artisan named Dennis Hopper was discovered to create an old-world lime wash paint treatment

"Designing the hotel was like Gershwin music, little staccatos of geometric figures, gold leaf and handmade, hand-painted furniture." Joszi Meskan, Chief Interior Designer

for the exterior stucco walls. It gave a subtle patina to both old and new construction. The old meeting rooms and kitchen were torn down to the dirt and rebuilt with new specifications. On any given day, hundreds of workers were on site

"What I get a reward out of is seeing how people love it," Ziebell says. "There are a number of details I might change looking back, but as a concept, it all held together and considering the enormous challenge we faced, it turned out as we envisioned it. Many people think the entire project is original, as if the renovation never happened. It's very rewarding hearing that."

From the very beginning, the Ungers had the notion of working with the Phoenix Chapter of the American Society

of Interior Designers. It was, after all, more akin to a great home than a hotel. The design society agreed.

The task for the designers—twenty-one individual teams in total—was not small: decorate and furnish fifteen casitas, formal reception rooms, the lobby, meeting rooms and T. Cook's, as well as several outdoor "rooms," at breakneck speed.

The general theme of the restoration was "Spanish Colonial Mediterranean." Each interior design team had to create a Mediterranean "feel" with local and regional influences, and to maintain a residential rather then commercial atmosphere. The design mantra was: "carry the character of the mansion throughout the property." The detailing had to respond to the tone set by the Cookes

A sitting area between arched paseos has painted palms adorning its ancient-looking walls. A birdcage from India stands in the corner.

A grand arrival sets the tone for the rest of a guest's stay.

exactly seventy-five years earlier. Even the large spaces, the ballrooms and meeting rooms, were to capture the essence of a great home. In addition, wherever possible, rooms should open up to the lavish, artful outdoor patios, reflecting pools and gardens. Of course, managing all this design creativity was a monumental task itself.

Smith, Ziebell, and Brown were given the job of orchestrating this symphony of design and construction. Immediately, the design team saw how the little "L"-shaped line of lodge-like guest rooms west of the mansion could be made luxurious with the simple additions of walled-in patios, both in front and in back of each suite. Ziebell added graceful arches to the new front entrances to support Smith's vision that all rooms and public spaces should have private patios and verandahs, like so many of the great European and Mexican estates.

Meskan was also in charge of décor for the new T. Cook's restaurant and coordinating buying trips to Peru, where much of the hotel's furniture was made. In addition, she was responsible for corralling a merry band of artisans to add the final artistic touches that made each room in the hotel distinct.

There are many stories about these artisans and how they made the hotel what it is today. There were two women from England, for example, who happened to be on holiday. Meskan knew of their work, tracked them down and coaxed them to fly to Phoenix. They were the experts in hand painting flowers (in a powerful, naïve style) on wood cabinetry and stone. Another artist, Willem Racke of San Francisco, was commissioned to put gold leaf stenciling on the walls in many of the rooms. Kim Sweet, brought to Royal Palms by reception and card room designer

Donna Vallone, painted cartouches in the Cervantes Room, reception, and lobby ceilings. Many were inspired by paintings found on the walls of churches in Mexico.

In the same way, another San Francisco-based artist, Roberta Ahrens, created an antique fantasy map for T. Cook's Lounge. Another artist, Hollywood set designer Pierre Clinton, came on board to create a set of oversized fireplace andirons and iron hood for the lounge fireplace. He then hammered out an aristocratic-looking family crest and placed it on the hood, as if it came from some enormous estancia.

The idea was to have everything in the hotel made by hand. Nothing was to be machine-made. In fact, Meskan found a furniture company in Peru with four hundred craftsmen willing to make new furniture – for every room in the hotel – by hand. She found Peruvian lamps, bought one and had Phoenix woodworkers reproduce it. She then hand-painted Spanish family crests on each lampshade. She found sets of ceramic, chinoiserie monkeys and placed them here and there in the lounge. In the lounge bookcase, she placed an authentic green cardinal's hat among the books.

The textiles and fabrics Meskan worked with were equally creative, bold and unusual. She relied heavily on specialist Louise Mann, a well-known textile designer.

Mann seemed to know instinctively what effect the restoration team wanted for the property. For example, in one sitting room off the main bar area Mann used the unusual but warm material of red leather squares for the flooring. Wall drapes were either a gauzy material or a canvas with off-white or gold and terracotta coloring. A white waffle weave material became bedding. A jazzy print was used for linens. The walls had the crinkly coloring of a brown paper bag. Mann liked designing and printing on "hopsacky" and canvas-like fabrics. She used ethnic images to draw inspiration for her designs, and then she added beads or fringe. Mann often would cut the bottom of fabric in strips at the hem, and then frayed it by hand. Mann also created two couches in this style.

Today, these fabrics, along with tableware and table linens, have been updated to offer guests an even greater and more luxurious sense of the Mediterranean feel the design team was originally after.

The hotel has an impressive art collection, too, but then it needed a large number of new pieces. Meskan was stumped as to where to get so much artwork needed for all the corridors, lounges, rooms, and restaurant.

One day while browsing in a Marin County antique store she came across a stack of portraits. Some were of "the saddest people" she had ever seen on canvas. Nevertheless, Meskan approached the owner, saying she had just a small budget to work within. The woman who owned the shop asked which portraits she liked. There were forty or more, but Meskan eyed the happier faces.

"I pointed to one with a nice face of a man," Meskan said.

"Six thousand," the proprietress said.

Meskan shook her head, no. The owner showed her a few more, with even more dour expressions. In the end, she bought twenty portraits, a combination of happy and severe faces.

Today, this eclectic "family" can be seen in T. Cook's private dining room.

The original hotel entrance on the east side of the building is still in use as an entry to and from the courtyard to the cactus garden.

The Montavista Collection

The new Montavista Collection of suites, terraces, and guestrooms are centered around the expansive Montavista Courtyard, where fountains, firepits, music, and lush gardens combine to create the ideal gathering place.

In January of 1998, the hotel was sold to Destination Hotels & Resorts, a distinctive collection of luxury, independent properties based out of Denver.

Senior executives from DH&R who pioneered the deal with Royal Palms understood how the fit of the hotel worked so well into the company's property portfolio. They asked Greg Miller to stay on and continue the job of creating a true five-star resort.

DH&R's first step was to strengthen the marketing and sales efforts. The first mission was to begin new branding and advertising campaigns. It was a challenge. There was a limited budget, little brand identity, no frequent guest program, no database, and they were in the most competitive resort market in the United States. Royal Palms was asking for top dollar rates against such venerable legends as The Boulders, The Biltmore, The Princess, The Hyatt Regency, The Camelback Inn, The Ritz Carlton and, its next-door neighbor, the opulent Phoenician.

"First and foremost, Destination Hotels & Resorts was committed to an extraordinary guest experience and to making sure the word got out about Royal Palms," Miller says. "Everyone knew this was a different kind of hotel. We just had to get the word out and stick to our mission."

It's been a fun ride for Greg Miller, both watching the hotel mature and seeing the occupancy rates outperform the competition in its category.

"We're fortunate to be the caretakers of this wonderful estate," says Miller of his work today. Miller and his team understand that what distinguishes the property from other resorts is its authenticity. The resort works hard at personalizing the experience for each guest and management encourages staff to take ownership.

"Our owners have a long-term vision of the property," says Miller. "We want to keep the historical integrity while enhancing the customer experience. This is an original and we have a high degree of respect for being stewards of this charming estate."

With over 330 associates year-round for 119 rooms (double the industry standard), guests are assured of feeling the personal touch at every turn.

Miller, now Vice President and Managing Director, and his staff live by one mantra: "Whatever it takes!" It seems to be working quite well.

The enhancement of the Cooke family's dream has continued long after the first building was planned back in 1926. Since the major renovation in the mid-1990's, Destination Hotels & Resorts has added many new features and amenities to the resort, including the world-class Alvadora Spa, an upgraded T. Cook's dining experience, and substantial improvements to the landscape design.

One of the many enticing views overlooking the Montevista Courtyard.

But most recently, the greatest enhancement has come with the complete re-design and renovation of the resort's southernmost structure, the original Plaza building, now called the Montavista Collection of guest rooms and suites.

With many luxury hotels in the area expanding, renovating, and new ones coming into the market, Royal Palms desired a consistent level of product throughout the property while also creating a competitive edge.

Though greatly improved during the first renovation, the Plaza building still held the largest number of rooms in the resort. Yet, despite its importance it received some of the least attention during the upgrade. As a result, some critical issues with the facility kept coming up, particularly the traffic noise from Camelback Road, interior sound-proofing, the master bath design and landscaping.

With the first renovation completed and the Alvadora Spa in operation, Destination Hotels & Resorts and Vice President and Managing Director Greg Miller decided it was time to meet these challenges head on, but to still create interiors that had a consistent match to the residential, unhurried feeling of the rest of the property.

Their first step was to go to back to the original restoration architect Don Zeibell of OZ Architects and interior designer Donna Vallone of Vallone Design. After some thinking and planning, Ziebell came back with a more radical approach: a major demolition of key sections of the building and a complete renovation from top to bottom.

It was a major change in design and budget, but the resort's management saw the wisdom of the overhaul, and its long-term benefits to the overall direction of the resort. But the time frame was tight: a little more than one year. And it was to be completed with minimal disturbance to guests enjoying the nearby pool. So, in January of 2006 work began.

"There were two objectives with Montavista," said Miller about the project. "One was to have the building and the

At sunset, Montevista guestrooms provide guests with romantic views of Camelback Mountain's ever changing colors

rooms blend with the rest of the resort and two, to have the majority of rooms face Camelback Mountain. Hence, the name Montavista."

The first action was the complete demolition of the center section of the building. This turned the building shape from a "W," with two narrow courtyards, to a "U," with a large central courtyard facing Camelback Mountain.

In the original structure many rooms faced south to busy Camelback Road and were accessed by a north facing corridor, which faced the mountain. The new design called for switching the corridor to the south side of the structure, facing the road, while the new rooms would face the mountains. This immediately solved the road noise issue.

"In effect, the least desired rooms suddenly became the most desired," said Ziebell of this re-configuring.

But even with these major hurdles tackled, the renovation became a far greater challenge than anticipated. There was an unexpected parking garage drainage issue, removal and re-assembly of an elevator, construction of a new, free-standing villa, now called the Alvadora Spa Villa, and the remaking of narrow guest rooms along the eastern and western sides into true four-star accommodations.

There were many other critical issues to be addressed, too, including better interior soundproofing, décor updates to match the rest of the resort, improved master bathrooms with separate showers and high-end fixtures, and transforming the new, larger courtyard into a series of intimate, welcoming seating areas with fire pits, fountains, and lush plantings.

The soundproofing alone called for three layers, a total of six layers between each room. As a result, the rooms

became so quiet that the fire inspector testing the alarms could not hear them. As a result, the team had to install individual annunciators in each room.

An unexpected structural issue, the courtyard drainage system, forced workers to spend an extra three weeks re-grading the patio down towards the mountain so as to facilitate drainage.

One idea that came to fruition was the idea of creating "spa terrace rooms" in the rooms unlike anything offered in the resort's other rooms. The plan was so well received by management that it was decided that the most desirable rooms, the center rooms, would be turned into a "collection" of these concept rooms. Each had gorgeous mountain views, luxurious European soaking tubs, and in-room massage and treatment amenities, as well as unique Asian and Zen-inspired decors. The idea was that the room was more about the spa experience than sleeping.

The rooms on the west side of the building were made larger by using the existing balconies for additional space, even though the rooms were spacious to start. Smaller "Romeo and Juliet" balconies were added to maintain an open-air feeling. On other second floor rooms, terraces were created to look down to the central courtyard, quickly becoming the defining feature of the structure. All rooms were given larger, spacious bathrooms, many with shutters opening to the bedroom, while others were given large living room areas, steam showers and fireplaces.

Based on her success on the resort's Alvadora Spa, Cervantes Library, and reception area, Vallone was challenged by management to infuse her caliber and style into the new guest rooms. Again, customized furniture and accents were found to personalize each room, as if

*"We want to keep the
historical integrity
while enhancing the
customer experience."*

guests were staying in a great private residence. Rooms were updated with flat panel televisions, fixtures in the bathroom were taken to the highest levels, and bathtubs were replaced with grand, over-sized European soaking tubs.

Vallone's trademark is her use of color, but in the Spa Terrace Rooms the idea was to cool the colors down. With the help of spa consultant Sylvia Sepielli of SPAd (Sylvia Planning And Design), the free-standing Alvadora Spa Villa and Spa Terrace Rooms intentionally departed from the resort's traditional Mediterranean look.

Today, this collection is centered around the Alvadora Spa Villa. At 1,300 square feet, it includes two bedrooms and a living area overlooking the courtyard on the south and the mountainside and pool area on the north. In addition, the Villa is immediately adjacent to the Alvadora Spa complex.

The Spa Terrace Rooms, of which there are six, are located within the Montavista structure and overlook the tiered garden courtyard, fire pits, and reflecting pool. Each room is quite spacious at 600 sq. ft. and offers sweeping mountain views.

The details of these rooms have been meticulously tailored to appeal to all senses and to create calmness and tranquility. For example, the dark wood flooring and chocolate brown leather furnishing, over-sized ottomans contrast with white linen draped four-poster daybed with sage, frosted violet, and white glass mosaic tiles, fresh flowers, intimate fireplace, reflective artwork, and French glass doors. The master bath features a European soaking tub with steam shower and luxurious linens.

The idea was that the benefits and pleasures of the Alvadora Spa were to be seamlessly transitioned into the comfort of the rooms, including offering such amenities as in-room dumbbells and yoga mat. Other special services include exclusive in-room spa treatments, sunrise and evening turndown rituals, and a daily "Intention of the Day."

"We believe The Montavista Collection is now consistent with the rest of the property, yet it offers guests some unique advantages, such as the panoramic views to Camelback Mountain, the newest touches in European-styled elegance, from linens to soaking tubs to bath fixtures, to private spa experiences, and have patios that look out onto the expansive courtyard," said Miller upon the Montavista's completion.

Opened in January 2007, this enclave of Mediterranean and Spa-inspired rooms now provides the resort with a new range of accommodations for guests. It also created a new "discovery space," a large, tranquil Montavista Courtyard with its reflecting pools, fountains, outdoor fireplaces, vibrant bougainvillea, and dramatic views. And in the evening there is another element of magic, too. As the sun sets upon Camelback Mountain, a serenade from a Spanish guitar comes alive for its guests.

The hotel's famous oval-shaped pool offers draped cabanas for the ultimate in pool-side privacy, just steps from the Montavista Courtyard. The resort's logo is captured in an elegant Mother of Pearl tile.

$\mathcal{A}$LVADORA

SPA at ROYAL PALMS

The entrance to Royal
Palms' Alvadora Spa,
a gateway to a healing
and sensory sanctuary.

*"The goal was to give each room
and area a different feel—
from Italian to Country
French to Spanish Colonial—
and to then reflect the
natural and organic
products and services that
the spa was offering."*

AT
ROYAL
PALMS

Alvadora Spa

Royal Palms Resort has always been a destination for romance and intimate escapes, but the Alvadora Spa takes this concept to an entirely different level. Alvadora stands alone as a healing and sensory sanctuary where guests immediately feel comfortable, relaxed, and at home.

Though built in 2002, Alvadora Spa has had from the beginning, the feeling that it has been part of the resort since its founding. Creating this sense was no easy task.

There were two primary objectives in building the Alvadora Spa. The first was to integrate the new amenity seamlessly into the rest of the property. The second was to continue to extend the residential feeling of the resort into the spa, while at the same time avoiding a sense of being "clinical."

One of the many open-air treatment rooms that continue the residential-feeling of the Royal Palms and sets the Alvadora Spa apart.

From the beginning, a great challenge in building the spa was that it was confined to the size of one old and little-used tennis court, situated on the far eastern side of the property. The space occupied some 7,200 sq. ft. and though it was not officially zoned as part of the "hotel" area, the city was pleased enough with what Royal Palms was doing with its restoration work that they "grandfathered" the location for additional hotel space, but only 6,200 sq. ft., a limited amount for a world-class spa.

Working within those restrictions, the design team of Don Ziebell of OZ Architects, interior designer Donna Vallone of Vallone Designs, and Cary Collier, of Collier & Collier Spas, noted spa consultants based in Whitefish, Montana, made the space look larger by organizing it around a series of Old World-inspired outdoor courtyards and upstairs treatment and exercise rooms.

Ziebell was selected as the architect because of his previous restoration work on the property while Vallone was selected once again because of her work on the original restoration of the Cervantes Library and the reception area. Collier came on board because of his world-renowned spa expertise. But the difference with Alvadora versus typical spa facilities, according to Greg Miller, general manager at the time, was to create a lighter blend of styles, more spiritual and inspiring, and to use the natural surroundings, views, gardens, open-air fireplaces—and to make it look authentically Mediterranean.

Two years in the making and much like the residential character of the resort, Alvadora Spa was designed from the start to be "residentially-oriented," according to Ziebell. The challenge throughout was to keep to the tough promise of making the Spa feel as if it were the same age as the rest of the property.

Enjoy a quiet moment in the Relaxation Room overlooking the courtyard.

As a result, many of the same artisans that worked on the original restoration were brought back to work on the Spa. For example, for surfaces, artist Dennis Hopper was brought back. Hopper was known for using a unique lime wash staining process that integrated four different layers of stain to the exterior walls, including air-brushed and artful designs, to create an Old World-look and perfectly match the existing resort finish. To create just the right patina, the polished concrete floors were stained four or more times and stairway tiles were selected to provide the authentic blend of Moorish and Spanish design. Rich color schemes of ochre and terracotta and natural stone reign throughout. Even the layered grout in the Acqua Dolce room was painstakingly applied to give guests a sense of Mediterranean authenticity.

In addition, the Spa incorporates not only many European influences, but Asian sensibilities too, making it truly international in scope.

The Spa's layout flows smoothly from one open-air room to another. The sight line from reception moves directly through the relaxation room through to the fountain-centered courtyard to the treatment rooms. The timbered courtyards and breezeways–never far from fragrant gardens and dappling Moorish-styled fountains –were purposely designed for the ideal natural "gateways" (rather than air-conditioned passageways) to the lounge areas, treatment rooms, and locker rooms. The upstairs areas included treatment rooms and the Fitness Centre, which were connected to the outdoors with open-air "windows" designed with the resort's north gardens and the changing colors of Camelback Mountain in mind.

*Manicures and pedicures are
provided under the soft lights
and in a soothing environment
of rich woods and fabrics.*

Each room in Alvadora has custom, faux-painted designs and original artwork, including murals depicting Delos Cooke and a map of the Old World. Artwork throughout includes beautiful vistas of the Tuscan countryside, pressed flowers behind glass, and Mexican folklorica. A beautiful Fleur De Lis fountain imported from France graces the entrance to the Spa while complementing the antique wooden hand-carved door. The goal: to give each room and area a different feel—from Italian to Country French to Spanish Colonial—and to reflect the natural and organic products and services approach that the spa was offering.

For guests entering the Spa for the first time, the first things that are noticed are the classical courtyards softened with pleasant, mind-relaxing water noise from fountains, the scented gardens, and the open, airy feeling for the treatments rooms, rather than the usual dark and closed-in spa spaces many facilities have. Even two large pedicure stations were built in the salon to face outside to the garden and pool area so guests can enjoy the view.

Signature treatments in the Spa include footbaths prior to treatment. So, in keeping with the style, the design team found special pottery bowls and pitchers to pour water in keeping with traditional methods and two vintage barber chairs were procured for the salon to add to the nostalgic experience.

Another example of taking spa design to the next level can be found in Acqua Dolce Villa. There, guests are treated to a special "waterfall shower" designed after a similar one found at the Grand Wailea's Terme Wailea Spa in Maui. The unique shower system, deluges guests at a rate of 30 gallons per minute.

The two showers, which hover side-by-side over custom-heated stone tables, needed quite a bit of testing, for height and water pressure, before being installed. Much of the testing happened in the architect's backyard. But the effort was worth it. Alvadora Spa offers its guests such luxurious hydration benefits.

Today, Alvadora Spa is where sophistication, elegance, Old World charm and lush gardens meet the modern wellness and fitness environment.

Within this private retreat, guests can experience a variety of luxurious treatments, including Terme Vivo (water therapies), Massaggio (massage), Corpo Terapia (body therapies), and Pella Cura (skin treatments).

The Spa, in its two levels, features seven treatment areas, two aesthetics rooms, four massage rooms, Acqua Dolce Villa, The Alvadora Salon for hair, nails, and makeup, and locker rooms with waterfall and rain-shower spas.

Acqua Dolce Villa, with its signature water treatment, deserves extra attention.

In this special series of rooms, guests (couples or singles) are indulged in the 90-minute Acqua Dolce Ritual. This treatment, among several offered, begins on the two custom-warmed stone tables as water cascades over the body from the unusual "cleansing" showers. Next, in the weightless world of a private Watsu pool a therapist provides a blissful, in-water deep-muscle massage, while the fragrances of the garden and wood fire fill the air. Then, guests proceed to the Minerale Bath and/or a

Botanica Bath, where either mineral or herbal therapy transports you to a deeper state of relaxation.

Alvadora offers a wide variety of treatments, services, and products, all resonating closely with the Mediterranean style of the resort. Treatments combine the natural ingredients found in the Mediterranean and the desert Southwest including herbs, flowers, oils and minerals with the highest standards of professional service.

The Spa has even developed a menu of citrus-based services designed to offer guests a "sense of place" that is far different from the typical desert-inspired treatments. The inspiration for this came from the on-site citrus grove within the resort's Valencia Gardens, a reminder of the thousands of acres of citrus trees that once flourished in the area.

The Spa's own fragrant orange blossom scent is quite fitting for the surroundings. The scent comes from neroli, the fragrant bitter orange blossom which produces one of the most cherished and expensive oils in the botanical kingdom. The neroli scent, named after the Princess of Nerola (near Rome) in the 17th Century, has been used for centuries in bridal bouquets to calm apprehension before the couple retired to the marriage bed. Today, the orange blossom represents joy, sensuality, weddings, and romance. As a result the Spa now offers another signature (and shared) 90-minute Citrus Ritual and series of other citrus-based treatments, including the Citrus Grove Facial, Orange Blossom Body Buff, and Simply Citrus Manicure/Pedicure.

In addition, Alvadora Spa includes a selection of other exotic, globally-inspired signature treatments, energy work, and other products from the Mediterranean, as well as a complete 24-hour Fitness Centre (with class activities and personal training available).

As an example of the "Massaggio" services available, the Spa offers the Renaissance Massage with Footbath, Aromatherapy Massage, Mare di Concha, Shiatsu, Deep Tissue, Couples, and Maternity massage, and many others. Body Treatments and Skin Care offer over dozens of different treatments, ranging from Citrus and Salt Foot Therapy to Olive Oil and Herb Facials to a Yogurt and Flower Body Treatment.

In addition, the Alvadora has its own signature scents, oils, and bath products collection, each having unique healing and nourishing properties that consist of organic herbs, flowers, fruits, oils, teas, and other ingredients indigenous to the Mediterranean. The collection balances life elements like water, fire, air, and earth.

The Fitness Centre is located adjacent to the Spa offering the latest in exercise equipment and aerobic activity. Regular classes are offered, including yoga and tai chi, on the unique "fitness terazzo" overlooking the pool and the tranquil Alegria Garden.

The Spa's treatments are designed to blend the simple wellness and healing solutions from both Europe and Asia, and Spa packages can be selected by guests as listed on the menu or can be custom-made for the day, over a weekend, or throughout a guest's stay.

A visit to the Alvadora Spa at Royal Palms is a spiritual and wellness experience as distinctive as the resort itself. To get to this private sanctuary, just follow the enchanting pathways that wind through the resort's private gardens and citrus groves – and then escape into the world of Alvadora.

Designer Casita 106 The Spanish Colonial theme comes to life in Deluxe Casita 106. An intricately carved stone fireplace mantle adds a Spanish flourish that is enhanced further with tile and stone insets. The room's colors are deep cranberry, emerald and cobalt. A carved mahogany canopy bed adds elegance and romance. The room affords a cushy seating area with a glass-topped, wrought-iron table and private patios both in front and in back of the casita. Designed by Janelle K. Schick, ASID, Schick Design Group.

"The goal throughout was to recreate
the romantic and charming
ambiance of the original
Mediterranean-style villa."

ROYAL
PALMS

Interiors

The Royal Palms restoration brought together some of the finest architects, builders, artisans, and designers in the Southwest. In one year, the hotel was gutted, rebuilt, and revived with the goal of re-creating the romantic ambiance of the original Mediterranean-style villa the Cookes built in the late 1920's. And, most recently, the resort saw the addition of the world-class Alvadora Spa and the new Montavista Collection of suites, guest rooms, and villa built to provide an even grander guest experience.

Throughout these changes the desire has been to create interiors that have a lived-in, unhurried feeling, yet without being over-stuffy. The restorers have sought a patina of antique furnishings, original artwork, hand-painted walls, and accessories worthy of a fine home. All the spaces at Royal Palms have that residential look and feel—from the entrance lobby to the guest suites and from the grounds to the pool and private courtyards—all were designed to create a captivating mood that entices guests to come back again and again.

Many of the guest casitas, now Designer Casitas, were expanded with the additions of front and back private and semi-private patios. Rooms, courtyards, and function rooms have all been enhanced with custom stenciling, new and old fixtures, refitted plumbing, and heating/cooling systems, but kept in the elegant style of the 1920's.

Even the meeting, banquet, and pre-function spaces were re-designed to have the cozy feeling of a home or private club. Wherever possible, these rooms open up to outdoor spaces, or "rooms," such as verandahs, lawns, courtyards, and reflecting pools, many with fireplaces or fountains as focal points.

With the additions of the Montavista Collection and Alvadora Spa, the resort makes the delicate balance of Old World charm and the best in 21st Century amenities.

A tour of Royal Palms finds colorful bougainvillea and jubilee-lined arcades leading to many quiet "discovery spaces," orange blossom-scented gardens, and warming outdoor fireplaces.

The best place to start the tour is at the front entrance to the old Cooke mansion, where the inspiration for the new Royal Palms first took hold.

Presidential Villa

Elegant enough for heads of state (President George W. Bush has stayed here several times), but instilled with an inviting sense of comfort, culture, and history, the Presidential Villa has many separate living and sitting areas, a dramatic fireplace and high ceilings. The villa is grand in scale and ideal for both formal and informal meetings. The large size of the villa is matched with deep, soft, oversized furnishings, and beautifully framed French glass doors leading to garden patios. The villa can be configured with one or two bedrooms. Designed by Sharon Fannin, ASID, Fannin Interiors

Camelback Villa

Part of the new construction during the hotel's restoration, the Camelback Villa is an executive suite with a dramatic wood-timbered ceiling and of a size perfect for business entertaining. The villa is known for its unique indoor-outdoor shower where guests can actually shower outdoors in a very private enclosed patio. Built-in bookcases, a long buffet, and distressed-leather club chairs in the large sitting area give the villa the feeling of a spacious, casual living room in a great southwestern home. Old World prints and Navajo rugs add an eclectic touch, a Royal Palms signature. Designed by Larry Lake, Inter Plan Design Group.

Honeymoon Villa

A romantic and dreamy setting, the Honeymoon Villa reflects the glamour of 1930's Mexico. A canopied bed fit for a wedding night is covered in gossamer fabrics and surrounded with pearlescent finishes and hand-carved, hand-painted Mexican furnishings. A leather-covered tea table reads: "Give me your hand Paloma, for this night you will sleep with me." The villa is accessorized with silver, wood and leather and in the sitting room stands a malachite-colored armoire hand-detailed with pink rose designs that were found in the hotel's gardens. Designed by Bruce Stodola, ASID, Bruce Stodola Interior Design.

Alvadora Spa Villa

A 1,300 sq. ft. two-bedroom and parlor suite, the Alvadora Spa Villa transcends luxury. A stand-alone villa, this unique accommodation offers a soothing Mediterranean décor highlighted with dark hardwood floors, crisp white linens, and accents of frosted sage and lavender. Located next to the Alvadora Spa and pool, the Spa Villa parlor has a comfortable seating area, expanded patio with intimate fireplace and a large flat screen television. Each bedroom has its own private bathroom featuring a European deep soaking tub, a stand-up indoor/outdoor steam shower, and private patios with outdoor fireplaces. Adding to the private spa experience, each room in the Villa is set up for in-room massage and spa treatments. Designed by Donna Vallone of Vallone Design.

Designer Casita 118

Like all the Designer Casitas, Number 18 is bungalow style and is located in the resort's lush Arcadia Gardens. This guest casita has a palm theme that can be seen from the framed prints on the walls to the fabrics on the massive, and romantic, canopy bed. French doors open to gardens and palms just beyond the private patio. The color scheme is done in soothing hues of cream, honey, and moss while the custom-made desk/nightstand allows guests a stimulating location for writing and a large flat screen TV for entertainment. Designed by Sylvia Lorts, Allied Member, ASID, Alexander/Sinclair.

Designer Casita 107 (right)

Inviting and cozy, the bold, rich color of red is the frame for this casita. With red walls and accents, the headboard is a hand-carved wood door set within an iron frame with the bed "serviced" by a unique "Carefree Cart," a rolling table that slides up the bed to make a romantic breakfast in bed for two. All the furniture is customized and hand-carved in the traditional styles of Mexico and Spain. Red silks and satins play off the walls, but lighter shades of camels and damasks give the room a feeling of openness. Designed by Sue Bickerdyke, Allied Member, ASID, and Joy Molever, Allied Member, ASID, of Sue Bickerdyke Interiors.

Designer Casita 115

Featuring rustic Old World style with warm tones ideal for the finest in living and relaxing, Designer Casita 115 has a grand sitting area with a stenciled fireplace as its central focal point. Gracious wrought-iron lighting as a romantic glow. French doors open to private patio gardens. With a custom designed armoire and eclectic accent pieces, this casita truly feels like a private residence. Designed by Sharon Fannin, ASID, Fannin Interiors.

Designer Casita 119 (left)

This Designer Casita is influenced by the warm colors and styles of the Mediterranean. Designed in the rich earth tones and bronzes of Tuscany, this guest casita is a casual place to relax, rest, and luxuriate. French doors open to a private patio and a crackling fire in the fireplace typifies the Royal Palms' essence of living in grand residential style. The walls are washed in an aged-yellow plaster and trimmed with inset diamond-shaped Old World emblems. Designed by Nancy L. Baserman-Vogel, ASID, Paul Berg Design.

Designer Casita 117

Spain's Andalusia region was the inspiration for this casita's décor. Richly textured and patterned carpets, custom wrought-iron fixtures, reading lamps, and tables, make this one of the resort's more intimate accommodations. Wood-shuttered French doors open to a bougainvillea-draped private patio. Over-sized, distressed leather chairs sit at the foot of a bed utilizing elements of limestone and pewter. Designed by Janelle K. Schick, ASID, Schick Design Group.

Valencia Casitas

The Valencia Casitas reside in the resort's Valencia Gardens and offer guests dramatic views of Camelback Mountain and breezes laced with citrus. At 450 sq. ft., the casitas are spacious enough to offer a quaint sitting area for two. A wrought-iron, four-poster king or queen bed with luxurious linens and fabrics add to this homey feel. Many come with fireplaces and all feature full-sized desks with flat screen televisions for work and entertainment. Designed by Donna Vallone of Vallone Design.

The Montavista Interiors

Alvadora Spa Terrace (left)

Located in the Montavista Enclave, the Alvadora Spa Terrace is a large 600 sq. ft. guestroom with views of reflecting pools and Camelback Mountain. Dark, wide-planked oak flooring and a white linen-draped four-poster daybed in the living area create an immediate sense of sanctuary. Custom-designed to offer an enchanting escape of self-discovery and deep relaxation, each Spa Terrace room is outfitted to offer private in-room spa treatments. Every detail has been tailored to appeal to all of the senses and create a venue for calmness and tranquility. Guests will find it in the hues of sage, frosted violet throughout, as well as in the color therapy lighting, fresh flowers, intimate fireplace, reflective artwork, and French glass doors. The master bath features a European soaking tub with steam shower, luxurious linens and reflexology slippers. Designed by Sylvia Sepielli of SPAd and Donna Vallone of Vallone Design.

Montavista Suites

The oversized 850 sq. ft. one-bedroom Montavista Suites (not shown) feature private terraces and patios with views to Camelback Mountain and the reflecting pools of the courtyard. A large separate living room area makes the suite grand enough for entertaining with friends or business associates. Creative design elements reflect a sense of enchantment and mystique in part through the interplay of fabric, finishes, and color. The master bedroom features a king bed and the master bathroom offers guests marble stone, a rustic wooden vanity, a European soaking tub, and a separate shower area that creates a sophisticated yet warm residential ambiance.

Valencia Suite

Terrace (right) & Estate Rooms (above)

Larger in size at 600 sq. ft. and also located in the Montavista enclave, the Valencia Suite has a residential ambience accented by deep, vibrant colors and bold patterns, upholstered headboard, stylish leather chair with ottoman, working desk, flat screen TV, and taupe-colored walls. The Valencia Suite offers guests an additional separate living room area with a queen sofa pullout, and an expansive, residential-style master bath with European soaking bath.

The Montavista Terrace & Estate Rooms, at nearly 500 sq. ft., offer additional space both in the king and double bed guest rooms. Terrace Rooms offer balconies or terraces with either mountain or garden views. Luxurious linens and separate soaking tub and shower add to the cozy feel in each, while a leather chair and ottoman, along with a full-sized desk and flat screen television, make these rooms ideal for romance, work, or both. The Estate Rooms have "Romeo and Juliet" balconies that open to either vistas or garden views. The master bath features a warm setting of soft cream marble stone, a rustic wooden vanity, European soaking tub and separate shower.

"The many beautiful, peaceful 'found spaces' are one of the great treasures for guests staying at Royal Palms"

Discovery Spaces

Since the early days of the Cookes, one of the key design elements running throughout Royal Palms is the concept of "discovery spaces," the small quiet areas (both inside and out) scattered among the property: citrus groves, quiet courtyards, the courtyard fountains, and outdoor gathering places around fireplaces.

With the addition of the Montavista Collection, a series of new outdoor living spaces have been added to the mix, too. These include new fountains, fire pits, and outdoor sitting areas in the Montavista Courtyard.

In addition, T. Cook's has enhanced its North Patio outdoor dining area with elegant, custom-made wrought-iron framed white canopies and cooling misters. In addition, its outdoor two-sided fireplace fills the evening with scented wood and the new heated floors beneath the bricks keep things cozy even on the coolest of nights.

In the pool, swimmers will discover new sparkling mother-of-pearl tiles and an inlay of the resort's famous logo while along the south-facing side new private cabanas, and lush landscaping provide a new air of elegance around the pool area.

In the original restoration, the idea was to enhance and expand on these "quiet surprises."

Today, one finds many examples of these quiet spaces throughout the property—a cantera stone fountain at the end of a long bougainvillea-draped corridor, a sitting area around a roaring mesquite wood fire, a private garden bench tucked among orange trees. These areas are considered "found spaces."

These meditative spots produce a kind of wonder that is unique to the hotel. In fact, the restoration called for an accompanying outdoor space for every meeting space. Indeed, virtually every indoor room is matched with an outdoor room or space of some kind, with glass French doors allowing for natural light.

The cozy fireplace and outdoor seating area off T. Cook's provides warmth and comfort. The tile orange tree mural dates to when the residence became a hotel and the dining room was called The Orange Tree.

The Cactus Garden at night.
Brick-paved walkways lead
around the garden and into
the old residence's mansion
courtyard. Many of the
bricks were collected from
pre-1900 Chicago buildings.

Starting with the central courtyard, with its Moorish-influenced reflecting pool, one can sit in this space many times and discover new things: the old Spanish tiles signifying provinces, the hidden away bas-relief bust of Christ, and the tile "Lady of Spain" mural.

One need only pass through the east entrance from the courtyard to the see the large Cactus Garden near T. Cook's outdoor dining area. This specimen garden contains a dozen different varieties of cacti: barrel, prickly pear, century, and spiky. The garden can be seen from the broad lawn or from a small sitting area around the patio's cozy outdoor fireplace. Above the fireplace is the well-known orange tree tile mural, with its one missing tile at the bottom left.

Above: Arched windows lighten and add an open feeling to a tower's wood ceiling.

Right: One of the many European crests found throughout the property.

Of course, one Cactus Garden is not enough. Alongside T. Cook's northern boundary there is a secluded large specimen cactus garden framed by one of the original brick and adobe walls. One giant prickly pear cactus dates back to the days of the Cookes, over 75 years ago.

In the northeastern corner of the property, there is the Alegria Garden, a romantic idyll for wedding nuptials. The Alegria Garden is fully enclosed and has a cantera stone altar with classic balustrades and a broad green lawn for family gatherings or it can be a quiet spot to read a book.

Just outside Alegria, paths wind around the Valencia Croquet Lawn. Cut from remnants of the original citrus groves, the Valencia green space is like a private backyard. Twin palms rise up over the greensward like sweethearts. This is not too far from a quaint brick patio that features another softly bubbling fountain. Here and there, as if artfully tossed by nature, one sees ancient Mexican grinding stones settled among cactus.

Right: A quiet, secluded courtyard designed for inspiration and reflection.

Above: At night, the air is sweet with the aroma of burning mesquite from the many outdoor fireplaces.

Below: An arched walkway along the Vernadero Lawn

A hammock stretches between two of the original palm trees planted on the property by Florence Cooke.

The gardens throughout the property are cared for organically. No pesticides or herbicides are used anywhere. This healthier environment is not only good for the guests, but the hibiscus, jubilee, Bird of Paradise, and bougainvillea thrive in the "living" soil created by the landscape team. The team has created its own composting "tea" to make the soil rich with nutrients that keep the wide mix of tropical and desert plants healthy and in full bloom, and make for an irresistible oasis for the many hummingbirds hovering among the lush foliage.

Those lucky enough to stay in the Valencia Casitas surrounding the lawn have a private courtyard they can enter through an old mesquite wood doorway. A spacious brick patio with a small brick fountain makes guests feel like they have their own private enclave to enjoy.

Just behind the swimming pool, near the Valencia casitas, there is another quiet courtyard. Here one can find three stone lions spitting water into a fountain filled with reeds and lilies. The spouts from the lions' mouths create a soothing gurgle for those lounging in the adjacent patio.

Top: A stone lion's head fountain adds magic to a pond located near the Valencia Casitas.

Right: Bougainvillea adds its brightness throughout the grounds.

Along the corridor to the Palmera entryway one finds a large outdoor sitting area meant as a respite from the day's adventures. Here, there are eight large cushions resting on hand-carved benches imported from India. In one corner stands a man-sized wooden horse dating back to the 1500's. In the opposite corner, a tall, ornate wire birdcage rests.

Most of the outdoor paths, corridors, breezeways and armadas are supported by unique, round brick columns. These were specified by Don Ziebell and custom manufactured in Mexico for Royal Palms. These columns can be seen leading from all the main areas of the hotel, past the many discovery spaces and to the guest suites.

All the fountains and brick patios, many with circular or purposely irregular shapes, are antique and have the worn, whitish look of decades. Ziebell also made clever use of colored-cement borders in the front entrance to help expand the limited number of old stone pavers.

Though not a traditional "discovery space," the long reflecting pool off the Estrella Salon ballroom is flanked by two large cantera stone urns at either end and offers a quiet, covered sitting area for post-day briefings or cool reflection.

Throughout the property, guests need only step outside their rooms to make a discovery of their own, and call it theirs.

Above: Romantically set for a meal for two, a Valencia Casita's private patio offers a serene setting for relaxing.

Right: The rounded bricks for the columns were designed and made specifically for Royal Palms by craftsmen in Mexico.

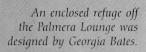

An enclosed refuge off
the Palmera Lounge was
designed by Georgia Bates.

"We want to keep the historical integrity while enhancing the customer experience. Royal Palms is an original and we have a high degree of respect for being stewards of this charming estate."

ROYAL
PALMS

Experience

The magic of Royal Palms lies in the intimacy of the estate. In fact, the entire focus of the "new" Royal Palms is to make sure guests have a highly personalized experience. Every detail has been considered to achieve this experience, from the relaxing Spanish guitar duets on the in-room stereo system to the ever-attendant staff to the remote-controlled fireplaces in casitas and villas.

Today, the hotel features one hundred and nineteen rooms, including Villas, Casitas, Suites and Estate Rooms. All are decorated by the best interior designers in Phoenix, and each guest suite is designed to feel like a room in a luxurious villa. Each offers those who visit the feeling as if they have arrived "home."

The rich colors, lush textures and rare artifacts create an intimacy that is rarely found in today's modern hotels. When people come to Royal Palms, they find a haven of romance, warmth, and serenity.

A Grand Entrance. The original mahagony wood doors, studded with ancient hand-forged clavos, open to reveal the magic of the central, Moorish-inspired courtyard and fountain. Tile carpet in entry designed by Donna Vallone of Vallone Design.

Since its restoration, the resort, restaurant and spa have received numerous industry awards, including Mobil Travel Guide's Four-Star Award, AAA Four-Diamond Award, Andrew Harper's Grand Award Winner and recognition in the 25th Annual Reader Survey of World's Best Hotels & Resorts. In 2008, Travel + Leisure awarded Royal Palms with the World's Best Awards ranking the property #76 hotel in the world and #23 in the U.S. and Canada. The resort is continuously recognized for its high caliber of service, romantic setting and attention to detail.

Despite the hotel's intimacy, it has twenty thousand square feet of distinctively designed, Spanish-influenced meeting space and its many "outdoor rooms" are ideal for groups, private dinners, weddings, and receptions of all sizes. All have the romantic flair of a grand estate. This sense is achieved through the artful use of antique accessories, intricate wrought-iron fixtures, grand fireplaces (both inside and outside) and, of course, inspiring views of Camelback Mountain.

For example, the Estrella Salon is spacious enough for a large formal reception of up to two hundred guests. The salon's interior features high, wood-beamed ceilings, wrought iron chandeliers and views of the lush, private Estrella Garden. It also has views out to the expansive reflecting pool (a former swimming pool for the old inn). In this part of the hotel, the old world ambiance is palpable.

Left: A former swimming pool, the reflecting pool is a romantic backdrop for both intimate and large gatherings.

Right: The Palmera Salon (above) and the Cervantes (below) are ideally suited for formal receptions, dinners, and executive meetings.

This hand carved fireplace in the Cervantes Lounge survived the Great Chicago Fire of 1871.

Courtyards are an intrical part of Royal Palms allowing for easy transition from indoors to outdoors.

Custom column capital designed exclusively for Royal Palms.

Another example of this charm can be found in the Palmera Salon. There, an elaborate fireplace, with an impressive hardwood mantle, anchors the room while another dramatic handcrafted iron chandelier hangs overhead and, just beyond, the sun or starlight dances in the reflecting pool. The Palmera Salon accommodates up to one hundred and twenty guests.

Royal Palms is recognized as a hotel with many great outdoor areas and "discovered" spaces.

One of the most charming is the Alegria Garden. This private courtyard on the property's far eastern boundary is enclosed by stone walls and surrounded by bright flowers and citrus trees. In the garden, an elevated stone platform is an ideal spot for wedding vows.

The lush Vernadero Lawn offers guests unfettered views of the changing colors of Camelback. Located just off the old Cooke Mansion's east wing, the lawn, with its imposing stone rams, is welcoming and has a wide variety of desert and Mediterranean plant life, including some of the property's original palm trees and an exotic cactus garden. It is an ideal setting for dinner, receptions, luncheons or large ceremonies.

Back inside, visitors can find a good book to read in the cozy Cervantes Lounge. The Library features an intricately carved fireplace that was once in the hotel's lobby. If the fireplace looks somewhat out of place due to its size, its intricately carved stonework, and formal nature it might be because it was originally from Charles Alberding's office in downtown Chicago.

Amber lit in the evening, the Vernadero Lawn sits between the original residence and the reflecting pool.

The story of the fireplace is a book in itself. The story goes that this grand hearth surround was one of the few things to survive The Great Chicago Fire of 1871. The old stone enclosure was located in a brownstone building facing the Water Tower on North Michigan Avenue. Like the fireplace, the Water Tower was one of the few structures standing from the conflagration caused by Mrs. O'Leary's clumsy cow.

Alberding had it taken apart, crated, shipped, and reassembled for Royal Palms. The combination of the big fireplace and cozy room makes for ideal dinners of between twenty and forty.

For romance seekers and honeymooners, the resort's experience is unmatched. From the moment one steps

Above: Like sentinels overseeing the Vernadero Lawn, custom carved stone rams designed by Greg Trutza are surrounded by orchid vine.

Left: Wood beam ceilings are visible throughout the property.

The fireplace that is the centerpiece
of the Cervantes Lounge survived
the Chicago Fire of 1871.

across the threshold and enters the central Moorish-influenced courtyard, it is clear this is no ordinary establishment. The glamour of a bygone era, when life was unhurried, is refined by management's commitment to elegance.

When you stay here you feel at home and comfortable while surrounded by hand-carved Mexican and European furnishings. In the Honeymoon Villa, even the inscription on the room's tea table embodies the hotel's spirit of romance: "Give me your hand Paloma, for this night you will sleep with me."

Great Service. Award winning dining. Elegant, romantic accommodations. A spectacular setting. A Mediterranean spa. A classic mansion. A Royal Palms experience is something truly original and unforgettable.

Above: A canopied bed in the Honeymoon Villa.

Left: Ironwork details are found throughout the grounds.

Right: Camelback Mountain looks down on the original courtyard and fountain, updated by Greg Trutza, to be the centerpiece for Royal Palms.

The Setting for Signature Occasions

*"Small executive groups will
appreciate the intimate
boardroom facilities and
handsome library-like salons.
This is a very special
spot overseen by an
exceptionally gracious staff."
Andrew Harper's Hideaway Report*

*The Vernadero offers
elegant surroundings for
executive board meetings
and signature dinners.*

Royal Palms is known for its intimate surroundings. That feeling holds true for large groups, too. Whether it's for business or social gatherings (events up to two hundred people are handled comfortably), the grounds and function rooms of Royal Palms make all events something to remember.

There are twenty thousand square feet of unique meeting room space, all designed with the feeling of a grand residence, as well as a number of outdoor spaces for large and small, formal, and informal gatherings.

For weddings, the private Alegria Garden offers just the right romantic touch for one to take wedding vows. And the large reflecting pool, and the adjacent Vernadero Lawn, is the ideal post-ceremony reception area. With its tall wood-beamed ceilings and gracious furnishings, the Estrella Salon makes for the perfect formal dinner venue, its French doors opening to both an adjoining patio and courtyard with reflecting pool.

Royal Palms' front entrance (left) offers the perfect romantic backdrop for the ultimate wedding celebration. The hotel's versatile function rooms (above) are ideal for both intimate and large gatherings, but always with the sense of "being home."

The food preparation for private dinning events at Royal Palms is distinctive among most resorts. As a boutique property that has fewer events, Royal Palms is able to prepare "á la minute," resulting in food presented straight from the kitchen with all the quality and freshness of a meal served from the main restaurant, T. Cook's.

An alternative to larger, convention-oriented hotels, Royal Palms offers intimacy and stateliness in all its function rooms. There are formal boardrooms, comfortable libraries, and outdoor "rooms" that are both quiet and inspiring.

The Palmera Lounge is graciously appointed with oversized leather armchairs and is endlessly functional. It also has associated pre-function areas called the Palmera Patio and Garden. All are part of the Palmera Salon function room complex, which can hold small to medium-sized groups. Even within T. Cook's there is functionality for those small groups looking for intimate seating for private events and specially-themed occasions. Add to these surroundings state-of-the-art audio-visual services and luxury amenities and you have the perfect combination.

This degree of style and function is what led *Fortune* Magazine to call Royal Palms "the poshest business hotel in Phoenix."

Palmera Salon and Garden provide intimate settings for both large and small events.

"T. Cook's is all about
sharing and bringing
people together."

THE BEST
AT
T. COOK'S

Savoring & Sharing

T. Cook's Mediterranean-inspired cuisine is a reflection of our chefs' passion for the authentic – and new. The recipe for T. Cook's success is based on savoring great food, experiencing its rustic, Tuscan ambiance, and sharing life's many stories with friends and family. The atmosphere at T. Cook's is both lively and comfortable and though the chefs at T. Cook's have won many awards, perhaps the most important accolade comes when guests say dining at T. Cook's is like "coming home."

T. Cook's chefs are world-class, having appeared numerous times as guest chefs at New York's citadel of cuisine, the James Beard House, and on the nationally-broadcast television show, Iron Chef.

Throughout the day, T. Cook's chefs put on a show of culinary magic. The scent of wood-smoke captivates as flames touch spit-roasted chicken in the open-fire kitchen. Scallops are seared and placed in a bed of saffron gratin while nearby a classic Mediterranean paella simmers. Tableside, candlelit eyes shine with anticipation as spoons toss organic mixed greens and servers gently pour butternut squash soup. A deft hand places the finishing touch on gorgeous plates of pasta with mushrooms and veal osso buco with roasted vegetables.

You find special touches everywhere at T. Cook's, in the richness of muted earth tones in the linens and fabrics, in the use of rare truffle oil, or in a custom-designed wedding cake from our award-winning pastry chef. T. Cook's even features its own "Director of Romance," who ensures every nuance of a guest's experience is delivered in Royal Palms style.

These are just a few of the many ingredients that separate a standard dining experience from an extraordinary one. This is what takes T. Cook's to the top of its class.

The main room at T. Cook's allows guests to dine in casual elegance. T. Cook's has received many awards and accolades since opening including the #1 restaurant in Phoenix by Food and Wine Magazine.

The North Patio at T. Cook's provides the comfort of the stars, moon, and a romantic fire.

The chefs of T. Cook's meet each request with passion and a love for the culinary delights they prepare. As the sun sets in the dining room and on the outdoor patios, the warm Tuscan décor reflects its ties to the Sonoran Desert and the russet-colored Camelback Mountain. A pianist adds a layer of atmosphere with sophisticated jazz. At the front of the dining room, a fire crackles merrily. The room is inspired by hundreds of years of Southern European cooking tradition.

And at the end of a great meal, desserts, the finishing notes of an elaborate dining experience, stand on their own at T. Cook's.

T. Cook's pastry chefs have won numerous awards and accolades for their delightful creations. In fact, those with a craving for sumptuous sweets often visit T. Cook's just to sample these delicacies.

There is everything for the chocolate lover. Try the Passione d 'Amanti or the Chocolate Grand Marnier Truffle. Or perhaps a light Fragoline de Bosco finished off with an espresso and Sambuca Biscotti.

When it comes to that ultimate romantic event, a wedding, T. Cook's Executive Pastry Chef works closely with brides to create their own custom-designed wedding cake. In fact, T. Cook's wedding cakes are so well-regarded they have been featured in *Bride's Magazine*.

It's the first impression that counts. But at T. Cook's, where a magical dining experience has grown from a tradition of sharing, the dessert is a true grand finale.

T. Cook's lounge offers a romantic setting, extensive wine list, an intriguing menu and live entertainment overlooking the Mansion Courtyard.

T. COOK'S
Classic Recipes

"Food is our common ground,
a universal experience."
James Beard

Busy chefs prepare the
night's fare in what Andrew
Harper's Hideaway Report
calls the "Best Hotel/Resort
Restaurant in the World."

139

Strawberry and Mixed Green Salad

With Pear Vinaigrette

This salad has a great combination of textures and flavors, from the satisfying crunch of the almonds, to the subtle pear taste. Use good, aged balsamic vinegar and ripe fruit to achieve the desired balance of tartness and sweetness.

(Serves 4)

INGREDIENTS:

3 oz.	Sliced almonds
6 oz.	Fresh mozzarella
4 oz.	Strawberries
6 oz.	Mixed greens
	Salt and pepper to taste

PEAR VINAIGRETTE: MAKES 2 CUPS

1 tbsp.	Olive oil
1 lb.	Pears, peeled, cored and diced
1 tsp.	Shallots, peeled and sliced
1 tsp.	Sugar
1/3 cup	White balsamic vinegar
3/4 cup	Canola/olive oil blend
	Salt and white pepper to taste

METHOD FOR PEAR VINAIGRETTE:

Heat the olive oil in a saucepan over medium heat. Stir in the pears, shallots and sugar. Sauté until shallots are tender, about 3 minutes. Remove from heat and chill. Place vinegar and chilled pear mixture in a blender and puree until smooth. With the motor running, slowly drizzle in the oil until the mixture is thickened. Taste with a lettuce leaf and adjust with more vinegar or oil if desired. Season with salt and white pepper to taste.

METHOD FOR SALAD:

Heat the oven to 350 degrees. Spread the almonds on a baking sheet and until golden brown, about 5-7 minutes. Set aside to cool. Cut the mozzarella into small, even cubes. Hull the strawberries and thinly slice. Toss the mixed greens, almonds, mozzarella and strawberries with as much pear vinaigrette as desired and season with salt and pepper to taste. Divide salad between four chilled plates.

Risotto

Arborio rice turns creamy and takes on the flavors of the ingredients cooked with it. It is one of the simple pleasures of an epicurean life – when prepared well. The key is to be attentive and stir constantly. The addition of whipped cream enhances the natural creaminess of the rice while providing additional body to the dish.

(Serves 4)

INGREDIENTS:

1 1/2	Canola & Olive oil (75% Canola/25% Olive)
1/4 medium	Onion, diced
1 cup	Arborio rice
2 1/2 cups	Chicken stock, heated
2 tbsp.	Butter, unsalted, softened
1/4 cup	Grated Parmigiano-Reggiano cheese
1/4 cup	Heavy cream, whipped
	Salt and white pepper to taste

METHOD:

Heat the olive oil in a saucepan over medium heat. Sauté onion until almost translucent, about 3 minutes. Stir in rice and sauté until all the grains are coated with oil and the onions are translucent, another 3 minutes. Pour in 1/2 cup of chicken stock. Stir constantly with a wooden spoon until most of the stock is absorbed. Repeat this step until the rice has absorbed all of the chicken stock, and is creamy but still *al dente*. Stir in the butter and cheese until smooth. Remove from heat and fold in whipped cream. Season with salt and white pepper to taste.

Chef's Note: This recipe serves 4 as a starter. To serve as a main dish, double the ingredients.

Signature *of* Cook's
Basil Pesto

This versatile recipe can be used simply for dipping bread or coating your favorite pasta.

(Serves 4)

INGREDIENTS:

1 1/2 cups	Olive oil
2 tbsp.	Pine nuts, roasted
2	Garlic Cloves, peeled
8 oz.	Picked basil
2 oz.	Grated parmesan
	Salt and black pepper to taste
2 tbsp.	Fresh lemon juice

METHOD:

Start with the oil, lemon juice, pine nuts, and garlic in a blender or food processor. Slowly add the basil and all the cheese. Blend well and season to taste. Refrigerate any leftover product.

Spiced Butternut Squash Soup

A traditional soup generally served in the Fall, most can find good quality butternut squash year-round. The savory ingredients of this preparation balance the sweetness of the squash and provide complexity not typically associated with this dish.

(Serves 6)

INGREDIENTS:

1 tbsp.	Olive oil
1 large	Carrot, peeled and diced
1 medium	Onion, peeled and diced
1 tbsp.	Ginger, fresh, peeled and minced
1 clove	Garlic, minced
2 1/4 lbs.	Butternut squash, peeled and large diced
4 cups	Chicken stock or water
1 cup	Heavy cream
3/4 tsp.	Cinnamon
1/2 tsp.	Nutmeg
1/2 cup	Pepitas (green pumpkin seeds), toasted
2 tbsp.	Pumpkin seed oil
	Salt and white pepper to taste

METHOD:

Heat olive oil in a stockpot over medium heat. Sauté the carrot, onion, ginger and garlic until the onions begin to soften, about 5 minutes. Stir in the butternut squash and cook another 5 minutes, stirring occasionally to prevent sticking. Pour in the stock or water, turn up the heat and bring to a boil. Reduce heat to a simmer and cook until the carrots and butternut squash are soft, about 20 minutes, stirring occasionally.

Stir in the cream and spices and cook just until cream is heated. Puree the soup until smooth with a hand-held blender, or in a full-size blender, in batches, filling only half-full each time. Be careful when pureeing hot liquid as it tends to escape from the blender. Season with salt and white pepper to taste and, if desired, strain soup through a fine mesh strainer. Divide soup evenly between 6 warmed bowls. Garnish with pepitas and a drizzle of pumpkin seed oil.

Pasta with Mushrooms and Truffle Oil

This recipe epitomizes the idea of "simple ingredients prepared well." Truffle oil enhances the earthiness of the mushrooms and asparagus while providing ample flavor and texture for the fresh pasta.

(Serves 4)

FRESH PASTA INGREDIENTS:

3-4 cups	Bread flour
4 large	Eggs
2 large	Egg yolks
2 tbsp.	Olive oil, divided

DISH INGREDIENTS:

10-12	Asparagus spears, trimmed
1 tbsp.	Olive oil
8 oz.	Fresh mushrooms (assortment), cleaned and chopped
2 cloves	Garlic, peeled and sliced
1 medium	Shallot, peeled and sliced
3 oz.	Cherry tomatoes, sliced in half
1 lb.	Cooked fresh pasta
2 tbsp.	Butter, unsalted
4 tsp.	Truffle oil
1/4 cup	Grated Parmigiano-Reggiano
	Truffle, shaved (if available)
	Salt and pepper to taste

Chef's Note: To create the texture shown in the photo, add 1 tablespoon of mushroom powder.

METHOD FOR PASTA DOUGH:

MIX BY HAND: Mound 3 cups of flour on a work surface. Make a well in the center. Beat the eggs, yolks and 4-1/2 teaspoons olive oil in a medium bowl. Pour into the center of the well. Pull the flour in over the egg mixture with a fork, slowly and intermittently until all the flour is mixed in. If dough is sticky, add more flour by the tablespoon. Knead dough until smooth and elastic, about 10 minutes. Cut dough in half and gather each half into a tight disk. Wrap in plastic and rest for about an hour in the refrigerator.

MIX WITH FOOD PROCESSOR: Place 3 cups of flour in the bowl of a food processor fitted with the metal blade. Place eggs, yolks and olive oil on top of flour. Pulse a few times to mix the ingredients and then process until the mixture resembles bread crumbs, about 30 seconds. Take the dough out of the bowl, place on a lightly floured work surface. If dough is sticky, add more flour by the tablespoon. Knead dough by hand until smooth and elastic, about 5 minutes. Cut dough in half and gather each half into a tight disk. Wrap in plastic and rest for about an hour in the refrigerator.

METHOD FOR ROLLING & COOKING PASTA DOUGH:

Cut the pasta dough into 1-inch thick strips. Work with one piece at a time, keeping remaining dough covered with plastic. Set the pasta machine on the widest setting and flatten the dough into a rectangular disc.

RECIPE CONTINUED ON APPENDIX PAGE 170

Mediterranean Paella

A feast featuring a medley of textures and flavors from both land and sea, this paella de-emphasizes the rice bringing the shellfish and sausage flavors forward.

(Serves 4)

RICE:

1 tbsp.	Olive oil
1/4 medium	Onion, peeled and diced
1 cup	Medium grain rice (Calasparra or Arborio)
2 cups	Chicken stock
Pinch	Saffron

PAELLA:

2 tbsp.	Olive oil
3-4 cloves	Garlic, peeled sliced
4	Live small clams or cockles, cleaned
2 large	Tomatoes, cored and diced
1 large	Red bell pepper, cored and diced
3 oz.	Spanish chorizo, sliced thickly
4 oz.	Cooked, diced pork loin
4 oz.	Cooked, shredded chicken breast
8	Live mussels, scrubbed
8	Shrimp (26/30 count), peeled and deveined
2 oz.	Calamari, cleaned and cut into 1/2 inch rings

1/4 cup	Chicken stock
1 sprig	Thyme, leaves only
1 sprig	Parsley, leaves only, chopped
2 tbsp.	Butter, unsalted
	Salt and pepper to taste

METHOD FOR RICE:

Heat the olive oil in a saucepan over medium-high heat. Stir in the onions and sauté about 2 minutes. Stir in the rice and cook until the grains are coated with oil. Stir in the chicken stock, saffron and a pinch of salt and pepper. Bring to a boil and then reduce the heat to a simmer. Cover and cook until the rice has absorbed all of the liquid, about 15 minutes. Let rest for 10 minutes, covered. Spread the rice out on a baking sheet to cool.

METHOD FOR PAELLA:

Heat 2 tablespoons of olive oil in a paella pan or 12-inch skillet. Sauté garlic quickly, 30 seconds, and then stir in clams (or cockles). Cook a couple of minutes, stirring constantly, and then stir in the tomatoes and red pepper. Cook a couple of minutes, stirring constantly and then stir in chorizo, pork loin, and chicken. Cook until tomatoes break down, a couple of minutes, and then stir in mussels and shrimp. Cook until shrimp are pink, stirring constantly, and then stir in the calamari rings. Cook about a minute and then stir in chicken stock, stirring to scrape up any browned bits on the bottom of the pan. Stir in reserved rice. Cook until heated through and then remove from heat. Stir in the herbs and butter until melted. Season with salt and pepper to taste.

Spit Roasted Chicken

With Goat Cheese Polenta Cake and Roasted Almonds

Perhaps the best (or most fail-safe) method of preparing chicken, spit-roasting allows the meat to self-baste, creating crispy, golden-brown skin and moist, perfectly cooked meat. Goat cheese gives the polenta a silky texture, while providing a tart counterpoint to the sweetness of the corn.

(Serves 4)

INGREDIENTS:

2 small	Chickens, about 2 1/2 pounds each
1 large	Carrot, peeled and cut in half crosswise
1 stalk	Celery, cut in half crosswise
1 medium	Onion, peeled and cut into quarters
1 head	Garlic, cut in half crosswise
4 sprigs	Thyme
	Salt and pepper
1/2 cup	Raw Marcona or other almonds
2 stalks	Celery, peeled
1/4 cup	Chicken stock
1 tbsp.	Butter, unsalted

POLENTA CAKES:

1 cup	Polenta, or coarse grain cornmeal
3 cups	Chicken stock
2 tbsp.	Butter, unsalted
1/4 cup	Goat cheese, crumbled
	Salt and white pepper

SAUCE:

2 cups	Chicken stock (preferably dark, homemade stock)
2 tbsp.	Butter, unsalted

METHOD FOR POLENTA CAKES:

Toast the polenta in a dry saucepan over medium heat, until fragrant, about 2 minutes. Pour in 1 cup of stock slowly, whisking constantly to avoid lumps. Whisk in remaining stock and whisk frequently until polenta is very thick and creamy. Polenta should be mostly smooth, not gritty. Stir in butter and goat cheese until smooth. Remove from heat and season with salt and white pepper. Line a 9 x 9 baking dish with plastic wrap. Pour polenta into lined pan and smooth top to an even thickness. Place in the refrigerator to chill and set. Cut chilled polenta into rounds with a 3-inch cookie cutter or cut into 3-inch squares. Reserve 4 polenta cakes for this dish and save the remaining cakes for another use.

METHOD FOR DISH:

Rinse and pat dry chickens. Trim excess fat and season the cavity with salt and pepper. Stuff each chicken with half a carrot, celery half, 2 onion quarters, half a garlic head and 2 thyme sprigs. Season the outside of the chicken with salt and pepper, and truss the chicken with butcher's twine in order to ensure even cooking. Slide the chickens onto the spit and rotisserie the chicken over pecan wood (or on a gas grill rotisserie with smoking pecan or hickory wood chips) until the outside is crispy and the internal thigh temperature reaches 160 degrees, about 1 to 1-1/4 hours.

RECIPE CONTINUED ON APPENDIX PAGE 170

Pan Roasted Scallops

With Saffron Gratin

Saffron provides an other-world backdrop for this simple, elegant scallop preparation. A nice acidic counterpoint is added by the tomato vinaigrette bringing out the round, rich flavors of the scallops and potato.

(Serves 4)

INGREDIENTS:

8 oz.	Green beans, trimmed and blanched*
1 tbsp.	Butter, unsalted
16	Sea scallops, tough muscle removed
2 tbsp.	Canola oil
Pinch	Sea salt

SAFFRON GRATIN:

1 lb.	Yukon gold potatoes, peeled and sliced 1/8-inch thick
1 cup	Heavy cream
Pinch	Saffron
	Salt and pepper to taste

TOMATO VINAIGRETTE:

1/4 cup	Extra virgin olive oil
1 medium	Shallot, peeled and finely diced
1 medium	Tomato, cored, seeded and finely diced
1/4 cup	Olives (assorted), pitted and finely diced
5 tbsp.	Sherry vinegar
	Salt and pepper to taste

METHOD FOR GRATIN:

Heat the oven to 350 degrees. Oil a 9 x 5 loaf pan and layer potatoes until all the potatoes are in the dish, seasoning with salt and pepper between each layer. Place the cream and saffron in a small saucepan and bring to a full boil. Remove from heat and pour cream over the potatoes. Bake uncovered for 35-40 minutes or until a knife slides easily through all layers. Remove from oven and cool. Chill in the refrigerator until cold, about 3 hours.

METHOD FOR VINAIGRETTE:

Heat the oil in a small saucepan over medium heat. Stir in the shallots and cook until shallots are tender, about 3 minutes. Whisk in the vinegar and remove from heat. Stir in the tomatoes and olives, and season with salt and pepper to taste. Keep warm.

METHOD FOR SCALLOPS:

Cut the blanched beans in half lengthwise (French cut). Cut each half into 2-inch pieces on the bias. Melt butter in a skillet over medium-high heat. Stir in green beans and cook until heated through and crisp-tender, about 3 minutes. Season with salt and pepper and keep warm. Pat the scallops dry with a paper towel and season with sea salt. Heat 1 tbsp. of canola oil in a large skillet over medium-high heat. Sear half the scallops when the oil is extremely hot, almost smoking, until golden brown, about a minute or so. Turn scallops over and sear other side for another minute or two. Both sides should be golden brown and cooked about medium rare. Remove from the pan and rest a couple of minutes. Repeat with remaining scallops, using the remaining 1 tablespoon of oil.

RECIPE CONTINUED ON APPENDIX PAGE 170

Veal Osso Bucco *With Roasted Vegetables*

Of Northern Italian origin, Osso Bucco is traditionally a hearty winter dish, though is now enjoyed year round. When roasted, veal shanks release a gelatin into the cooking liquid creating a velvety-smooth sauce that rivals any butter sauce. The veal becomes fork tender, taking on the flavors of the braising liquid.

(Serves 4)

INGREDIENTS:

4	Veal shanks (or lamb), 1 pound each
	Salt and pepper
1/2 cup	Flour, all-purpose
4 tbsp.	Canola oil
1 medium	Onion, diced
3 cloves	Garlic, minced
2 sprigs	Thyme
2 sprigs	Rosemary
1	Bay leaf
1 cup	White wine
4 medium	Tomatoes, cored and diced
1 tbsp.	Tomato paste
3 cups	Veal or chicken stock
2 sprigs	Parsley, leaves only

ROASTED VEGETABLES:

3 large	Carrots, peeled
12 small	Shallots, peeled and trimmed
2 tbsp.	Olive oil
	Salt and pepper

METHOD FOR OSSO BUCCO:

Tie each shank with butcher's twine around the circumference to secure. Season shanks generously with salt and pepper and dredge in flour. Shake off excess. Heat the oil in a large Dutch oven over medium-high heat. Brown shanks on both flat sides, about 3 minutes each side. Remove from pot and set aside. Stir in the onion. Cook until almost translucent, about 3 minutes and then stir in garlic, thyme, rosemary and bay leaf. Cook another minute, and pour in the wine, stirring to scrape up any brown bits. Cook until only 1/3 cup of wine remains, about 5 minutes. Stir in the tomatoes and tomato paste. Cook until tomatoes begin to break down, about 2 minutes. Nestle the shanks into the pot. Pour in the stock and bring to a boil. Reduce the heat to a simmer and cover the pot. Simmer on low heat until meat is extremely tender and falling off the bone, about 2 to 2 1/2 hours. Remove the shanks and set aside, loosely covered. Turn the heat to medium-high and reduce the braising liquid until it coats the back of the spoon, about 15-20 minutes. Remove the thyme, rosemary and bay leaf. Strain the sauce if desired. Taste and season with salt and pepper if desired.

METHOD FOR VEGETABLES:

Heat the oven to 350 degrees. Cut carrots crosswise into 3 equal pieces, and then cut each piece in half lengthwise. Toss the whole shallots and carrots with the oil and season with salt and pepper. Place on a lined baking sheet and roast until tender and lightly browned, about 30 minutes.

RECIPE CONTINUED ON APPENDIX PAGE 170

Pan Roasted Cod

With a Crab and Red Pepper Tart

Cod prepared this way will have a beautiful, crispy, caramelized exterior with a flaky, moist, slightly opaque interior. The tart marries the flavors of a classic crab cake with a lightly crunchy pastry, and is enhanced by an elegant vermouth sauce.

(Serves 4)

INGREDIENTS:

4	Cod fillets, 6 oz. each, skin-on preferably
2 tbsp.	Olive oil, divided
1 tsp.	Sea salt
2 bunches	Swiss chard, stems removed, roughly chopped
8	Teardrop or cherry tomatoes, sliced in half

TART SHELL:

8 oz.	Flour, all-purpose
Pinch	Salt
9 tbsp.	Butter, unsalted, chilled and diced
1 large	Egg, beaten
2 oz.	Water, cold

TART FILLING:

3/4 cup	Lump crab, picked through
1/2 small	Red bell pepper, cored and diced
3/4 cup	Grated Manchego cheese (or other hard cheese)
3 large	Eggs
2/3 cup	Half and Half
1/2 tsp.	Salt
Pinch	White pepper

SAUCE:

2 oz.	Dry vermouth
1 cup	Fish or chicken stock
1 cup	Heavy cream
	Salt and white pepper to taste

METHOD FOR TART SHELL:

Place the flour, salt and chilled butter in a food processor and pulse until it resembles coarse meal. Transfer mixture to a large bowl. Stir in the egg and water until the dough just comes together. Flatten into a disk and wrap in plastic wrap. Refrigerate for at least an hour. Heat the oven to 350 degrees. Remove dough from the refrigerator and divide into 4 equal pieces. Roll each piece into a circle on a lightly floured work surface until it is about 1/8-inch thick. Lift and place in a 4-inch tart mold with a removable bottom, pressing onto bottom and sides, with dough extending about 1/2 inch above the sides of the mold. Place a piece of parchment paper slightly larger than mold on top and fill with beans or pie weights. Repeat with remaining tart dough. Place tarts on a baking sheet and bake about 20 minutes (dough will not be done and will shrink). Remove from the oven and cool. Remove weights and parchment paper.

METHOD FOR TART FILLING:

Heat the oven to 350 degrees. Toss the crab and red pepper together and evenly distribute among the tarts. Sprinkle each tart evenly with cheese. Do not press the cheese into the tart. Beat the eggs with Half and Half and salt and pepper.

RECIPE CONTINUED ON APPENDIX PAGE 170

Grilled Beef Tenderloin

With Mushroom, Potato Galette and Grilled Scallions

A classic beef dish with a contemporary twist, the simplified bordelaise sauce with bacon enhances the smokey richness of the grilled meat, while rounding out the potato and mushroom flavors.

(Serves 4)

INGREDIENTS:

4 filets	Beef tenderloin, 6 oz. each
16	Scallions, washed and trimmed
1 tbsp.	Olive oil, divided
1 large	Carrot, peeled and diced
1/4 cup	Chicken stock
1 tsp.	Butter, unsalted
	Salt and pepper to taste

GALETTE:

1 lb.	Yukon Gold potatoes
2 tbsp.	Butter, unsalted
1 tbsp.	Olive oil
6 oz.	Assorted mushrooms, cleaned and chopped
2 tsp.	Chopped fresh tarragon
	Salt and pepper to taste

SAUCE:

1 slice	Bacon, diced
1/4 medium	Onion, diced
1/4 stalk	Celery, diced
1/4 large	Carrot, peeled and diced
1 clove	Garlic, minced
2 oz.	Madeira
1 cup	Veal demi-glace

METHOD FOR SAUCE:

Cook the bacon in a saucepan over medium heat until browned. Stir in vegetables and garlic. Cook until onions are almost translucent, about 3 minutes. Pour in Madeira and reduce until almost dry. Stir in demi-glace and simmer until the sauce coats the back of a spoon, about 10 minutes. Strain through a fine mesh sieve.

METHOD FOR GALETTE:

Boil the potatoes until tender. Remove and cool slightly. When cool enough to handle but still warm, peel and mash with butter until smooth. Meanwhile, heat 1 tablespoon olive oil in a large skillet over medium heat. Cook mushrooms until tender, about 8 minutes. Stir in tarragon and mashed potatoes. Season with salt and pepper to taste. Heat the oven to 350 degrees. Place 4 (3-inch) ring molds on a lined baking sheet. Brush molds with olive oil and divide the potato mixture evenly between the 4 molds, pressing down to form a compact cake. Brush the tops with olive oil and bake until heated through, about 15 minutes.

METHOD FOR BEEF FILETS:

Heat a grill to medium-high heat. Season the filets with salt and pepper. Grill the filets until medium rare (130 degrees), about 10-12 minutes, turning once halfway through. Remove from grill and cover loosely with foil to keep warm. While the beef is on the grill, toss the scallions with salt and 2 teaspoons of olive oil. Place on the grill off direct heat until soft and wilted, about 5 minutes.

RECIPE CONTINUED ON APPENDIX PAGE 171

*"You don't have to cook
fancy or complicated
masterpieces – just good food
from fresh ingredients."*
Julia Child

T. COOK'S
Just Desserts

*Please see the Appendix
for this truffle recipe.*

Passione d'Amanti

Passion, as in passion fruit, is but one of the fruits used to make this amazing amalgamation of berries, chocolate and brie.

(Serves 10)

CHOCOLATE TORTE:

1 cup	Sugar
1 cup	Brown sugar
8 tbsp.	Butter, unsalted
4 oz.	Semisweet chocolate, chopped
2 large	Eggs
2 cups	Pastry flour
1/4 cup	Cocoa powder
1 tsp.	Vanilla extract
1 cup	Whole milk

FRUIT SAUCE:

3 cups	Passion fruit puree (or pineapple, or mango)
1 cup	Sugar

MOUSSE:

1/2 cup	Fruit sauce
4 oz.	Brie cheese, rind removed & room temperature
6 oz.	White chocolate, chopped
2 cups	Heavy cream, whipped to soft peaks

GARNISHES:

1/4 cup	Sugar
1 sprig	Mint, leaves only
1 pint	Blueberries
1 pint	Blackberries
1 pint	Raspberries
	Powdered sugar
	Large martini glasses

METHOD FOR TORTE:

Heat the oven to 350 degrees. Place the sugars and butter in a small saucepan over low heat. Stir until butter is melted. Pour into a mixer fitted with a paddle attachment. Sprinkle chocolate on top and mix just until chocolate is melted. Beat in the eggs until smooth. Sift pastry flour and cocoa together. Sprinkle on top of batter. Mix on low speed just until smooth, stopping to scrape the sides of the bowl once. Pour in vanilla and milk and mix on low speed just until smooth. Batter will be very liquid. Line an 18 x 13 x 1 baking sheet (half sheet pan) with parchment paper. Pour batter into pan and spread batter to edges. Smooth to an even thickness. Bake until firm on top, about 12 minutes. Remove from oven and cool. Chill (or freeze), and then cut out 35 rounds, using a 2-inch cookie cutter. Reserve 10 for this dessert and freeze the remaining for another use.

METHOD FOR FRUIT SAUCE:

Place fruit puree and sugar in a wide saucepan over medium heat. Bring to a boil and reduce to a simmer. Cook puree, stirring occasionally, until mixture is reduced by half. Remove from heat and pour into a bowl set inside a larger bowl of ice water to chill. Refrigerate, covered, until needed.

METHOD FOR MOUSSE:

Place 1/2 cup fruit sauce (reserve remaining sauce for composing the dessert) in a blender. Top with brie chunks and blend until smooth. Place white chocolate in a double boiler over low heat. Stir just until melted. Remove from heat. Stir brie mixture into melted white chocolate. Fold in about 1/4 of the whipped cream to lighten the mixture. Fold in the remaining whipped cream until smooth. Chill until needed.

RECIPE CONTINUED ON APPENDIX PAGE 171

Chocolate Flourless Torte

With Orange Supreme and Cointreau Butter

A classic combination of citrus flavors and rich chocolate, this torte lends itself well to finishing traditional holiday meals.

(Serves 8)

INGREDIENTS:

9 tbsp.	Butter, unsalted, softened, divided
12 oz.	Semisweet chocolate (72% cacao), chopped
6 large	Eggs
1/4 cup	Sugar
2 large	Oranges, peeled and segmented

COINTREAU BUTTER SAUCE:

8 tbsp.	Butter, unsalted
1/2 cup	Brown sugar
1/2 cup	Cointreau liqueur
1 tbsp.	Orange juice
1 cup	Heavy cream

Chef's Note:
Add a scoop of vanilla bean ice cream for even more decadence.

METHOD FOR TORTE:

Heat the oven to 350 degrees. Butter 8 (4 oz.) ramekins with 1 tablespoon of butter and place in a roasting pan. Set aside. Melt remaining butter and chocolate in a double boiler over low heat, stirring until the chocolate is melted. Remove from heat. Beat eggs and sugar together in a mixing bowl until thick and smooth. Beat egg mixture into the melted chocolate until smooth. Pour batter into ramekins, about 3/4's full. Place ramekins in the oven. Pour enough hot water into the roasting pan to come halfway up the sides of the ramekins. Bake uncovered until tortes are puffed and just slightly pull away from the edges, about 22-25 minutes. Remove from the oven and the water bath. Run a knife around the edges of the ramekins. Cool 5-10 minutes. Line a baking sheet with parchment paper. Unmold tortes by turning the ramekins upside down onto parchment paper and tapping until cakes release.

METHOD FOR SAUCE:

Place the butter, brown sugar, Cointreau and orange juice in a small sauce pan over medium heat. Bring to a rolling boil and cook for 5 minutes. Stir in heavy cream and boil an additional 2 minutes. Remove from heat and set pan in a bowl of ice water to chill.

COMPOSING THE DESSERT:

Reheat tortes in a 200-degree oven if necessary, until warm. Place torte in the center of a dessert plate. Drizzle with butter sauce, and scatter orange segments around plate.

Fragoline di Bosco

Strawberries, melon and tarragon make for a light, refreshingly herbaceous dessert ideal for finishing off a warm weather meal.

(Serves 4)

FRAGOLINE:

3/4 cup	Muscato D'Asti (Nivole or other brand)
2 tbsp.	Honey
1/4 cup	Tarragon leaves, chopped
1 pound	Strawberries, hulled and chopped
1/2 cup	Small honeydew balls
1/2 cup	Small cantaloupe balls
1 cup	Almond Streusel or crushed Amaretti cookies
4 scoops	Lemon gelato

ALMOND STREUSEL:

2 oz.	Almond paste
4 1/2 oz.	Sugar
8 tbsp.	Butter, unsalted
3/4 tsp.	Vanilla extract
6 oz.	Bread flour
1 tbsp.	Cinnamon

GARNISHES:

1/2 cup	Almond streusel or crushed amaretti cookies
1 sprig	Tarragon, leaves only
4 scoops	Lemon gelato

METHOD FOR FRAGOLINE:

Whisk wine and honey together until smooth. Stir in tarragon. Toss strawberries and melons with wine mixture. Refrigerate for 1 hour.

METHOD FOR STREUSEL:

Heat the oven to 350 degrees. Beat almond paste, sugar, butter and vanilla extract in a mixer with a paddle attachment on medium speed just until smooth, stopping to scrape down the sides of the bowl once. Sprinkle flour and cinnamon on top of mixture and mix on low speed just until combined. Mixture should be dry and crumbly. Line a small baking sheet with parchment paper and spread streusel in a thin layer (do not press down). Bake until golden brown, about 20 minutes. Remove from oven and cool slightly. Crumble by hand in a food processor. Set aside.

COMPOSING THE DESSERT:

Place a ring mold (2 1/2 inches wide by 2 inches high) in the center of a plate. Strain the fruit mixture, reserving the syrup. Toss fruit with 1 cup of crumbled almond streusel (or amaretti). Pack about 1/2 cup of fruit mixture into the mold. Remove the ring mold. Spoon reserved syrup around the tower. Place a small scoop of gelato on top and lay a few tarragon leaves on the gelato. Repeat with remaining plates.

Sambuca Biscotti

"Biscotti" literally means to "cook twice". This method is what produces the deliciously crunchy cookie that many like to enjoy with coffee-based drinks. In Italy, Sambuca is often added to coffee, so this may be the perfect biscotti to enjoy with your after-dinner espresso.

(Makes 3 dozen)

INGREDIENTS:

8 tbsp.	Butter, unsalted
6 oz.	Sugar
2 large	Eggs
3 tbsp.	Sambuca liqueur
1/2 tsp.	Vanilla extract
7 oz.	Bread Flour
2 oz.	Whole wheat flour
1 tsp.	Baking powder
1/2 tsp.	Salt
3 oz.	Dried apricots (cranberries or cherries), chopped
3 oz.	Pistachios (or almonds or pecans), chopped

METHOD:

Heat the oven to 325 degrees. Beat the butter and sugar together in a mixer fitted with a paddle until light and fluffy. Whisk eggs with Sambuca and vanilla in a medium mixing bowl. Pour eggs over butter mixture and beat until smooth, stopping once to scrape the sides of the bowl. Whisk the flours, baking powder and salt together in another bowl. Sprinkle flour mixture over batter. Beat on low speed for 1 minute, and then increase speed to medium and mix until almost incorporated, but still crumbly. Sprinkle batter with dried fruit and nuts. Mix on low speed just until fruit and nuts are evenly distributed. Dust a work surface with a little flour. Scrape the sticky dough onto the work surface and divide in half. Flour your hands and pat each half into a rectangle about 1/2 inch thick, 3 inches wide and 10 inches long. Transfer dough to a parchment paper lined baking sheet and bake until firm on top and edges are light golden brown, about 25 minutes. Remove from oven and cool 5 minutes. Leave oven on. Cut biscotti into 1/4 to 1/2 inch slices. Lay biscotti, cut side up, on two baking sheets and bake until almost dry, about 12 minutes. Remove from oven and transfer biscotti to a cooling rack to cool.

Pasta CONTINUED FROM PAGE 147

Roll through the pasta machine several times, decreasing the setting with each roll, resulting in longer and thinner dough each time through. After dough has run through the lowest or next to lowest setting, it is ready to cut, either with the pasta machine cutter or by hand. Cut into desired shape. Lay pasta flat on a baking sheet and cover with plastic wrap. Repeat process with remaining dough. Bring a large pot of water to a boil. Stir in a couple tablespoons of salt and gradually add pasta strands, a handful at a time. Boil, stirring gently, until pasta is *al dente*, about 3 to 4 minutes. Drain and toss with remaining 1-1/2 teaspoons of olive oil to keep pasta from sticking.

METHOD FOR FINISHED DISH: Drop asparagus into a pot of boiling, salted water for 2 minutes. Remove from boiling water and plunge the asparagus into a bowl of ice water to stop the cooking. Remove when cool and pat dry. Cut each spear into 2-inch pieces, at an angle. Set aside. Heat 1 tablespoon of olive oil in a large skillet. Stir in the mushrooms, garlic and shallot. Cook until mushrooms are almost tender, about 5 minutes. Stir in the asparagus and tomatoes and cook another minute. Stir in the pasta and cook until heated through. Stir in the butter until melted. Season with salt and pepper to taste. Divide mixture among 4 warmed pasta bowls and drizzle each with a teaspoon of truffle oil. Sprinkle each with about 1 tablespoon of Parmigiano-Reggiano.

Spit Roasted Chicken CONTINUED FROM PAGE 151

Roast the almonds in a 350 degree oven until golden brown, about 5-7 minutes. Cut the celery at an extreme angle so that each piece, while only 1/4-inch thick, is about 3 inches long. Place celery in a small saucepan with chicken stock and butter. Bring to a boil and simmer until tender, about 5 minutes. Taste and season with salt.

METHOD FOR SAUCE: Bring the stock to a boil and reduce until 1/2 cup remains. Remove from heat and whisk in butter. Keep warm.

COMPOSING THE DISH: Heat the oven to 350 degrees. Place polenta on a lined baking sheet and reheat until hot, about 10 minutes. Place a warm polenta cake in the middle of

a warm plate. Place a thigh on top of the polenta. Rest a breast half, skin side up, against the thigh. Scatter almonds and celery around plate. Spoon sauce over chicken. (The chickens may be roasted in a preheated 350 degree oven if rotisserie is not available.) Remove from the spit or oven and rest for 15 minutes. Carve each breast half away from the bone, in one piece. Cut off each thigh (reserve legs and carcass for another use). Cover and keep warm.

Pan Roasted Scallops CONTINUED FROM PAGE 152

COMPOSING THE DISH: Heat the oven to 350 degrees. Cut gratin into four even rectangles and place on a lined baking sheet. Place in the oven until hot, about 10 minutes. Place the warmed gratin in the middle of the plate. Place the scallops on top and then arrange green beans on top of the scallops. Spoon the warm vinaigrette around the dish.

TO BLANCH BEANS: Drop beans in boiling water for about two minutes. Remove beans and plunge in a bowl of ice water to stop the cooking. Remove from ice water when cool, and pat dry before continuing.

Veal Osso Bucco CONTINUED FROM PAGE 155

COMPOSING THE DISH: Place a scoop of risotto (recipe on page 144) in the center of a warm plate. Scatter the vegetables around the risotto. Place a shank on top of the risotto and remove the twine. Spoon the sauce all over the shank. Garnish with parsley leaves.

Pan Roasted Cod CONTINUED FROM PAGE 156

Strain mixture through a fine sieve. Pour mixture evenly into the molds. Bake until just set, about 25 minutes. Remove from oven and cool for 30 minutes. Run a knife around the top of the tart to remove any excess pastry and remove from the molds. Place tarts on a small baking sheet. Refrigerate, uncovered, until completely chilled, about 2 hours. Cut each tart in half. Reserve 4 tart halves and save the remaining 4 for another use.

METHOD FOR SAUCE: Boil the vermouth in a small saucepan over medium-high heat until only 1 or 2 tablespoons remain. Stir in the stock and bring to a boil. Reduce until only

1/4 cup remains. Stir in the cream and reduce until only 2/3 cup remains. (Watch carefully; cream tends to boil over.) Taste and season with salt and white pepper to taste.

METHOD FOR FINISHING DISH: Heat the oven to 250 degrees. Place the tart halves on a baking sheet and warm in the oven until heated through, about 10 minutes. Heat 1 tablespoon of olive oil in a large, oven-proof skillet over medium-high heat until hot. Pat cod fillets dry with a paper towel and season with sea salt. Place cod, skin side up, in the skillet. Sear until light golden brown, about 3 minutes. Turn fillets over and place skillet in the oven until cod is just done, about 5 minutes. Remove skin before plating if desired. Heat the remaining 2 tablespoons of olive oil in a large skillet over medium high heat. Stir in the Swiss chard. Cook until wilted and tender. Season with salt and pepper to taste. Remove from heat and blot the chard with paper towels to remove excess moisture.

COMPOSING THE DISH: Place a tart half in the center of a warm plate and mound 1/4 of the chard in front of the tart. Prop cod up against tart, covering the chard and drizzle 1/4 of the cream sauce all around the tart. Place 4 tomato halves around tart.

Grilled Beef Tenderloin Continued From Page 159

Remove from grill and set aside. While the beef is resting, heat the remaining 1 teaspoon of olive oil and 1 teaspoon of butter in a small sauté pan over high heat. Stir in the carrots and cook 2-3 minutes. Stir in the chicken stock and reduce until the pan is almost dry, about 4 minutes. Season carrots with salt and pepper, and set aside.

COMPOSING THE DISH: Place the warm potato galette in the middle of a plate and remove the mold. Drizzle about 1/4 cup of sauce around the potato and scatter a few carrots around the sauce. Rest the beef on top of the potato. Fold scallions and place on top of beef.

Passione d'Amanti Continued From Page 163

COMPOSING THE DESSERT: Place the mint and sugar in a mortar. Muddle with the pestle until crumbly. Set aside. Dust the 10 chocolate torte circles with powdered sugar on both sides.

Set aside. Place a tablespoon of reserved fruit sauce in the bottom of a martini glass. Space 3 slices of strawberries around the bottom of the martini glass, touching the fruit sauce. Spoon a scant 1/2 cup of white chocolate mousse over sauce. Stand a torte circle on its side in the center of the mousse, lightly pressing the circle into the mousse so that it stands upright. Scatter mixed berries around the torte on top of the mousse. Spoon a little fruit sauce on berries and sprinkle with mint sugar.

Chocolate Grand Marnier Truffles

(Makes 25-30 truffles)

INGREDIENTS:

6 oz.	Semisweet chocolate, finely chopped
1/4 cup	Heavy cream
2 tbsp.	Butter, unsalted
2 tbsp.	Grand Marnier liqueur

COATING:

8 oz.	Semisweet chocolate, finely chopped

METHOD: Place chocolate in mixing bowl. Place cream and butter in a small saucepan over medium heat. Bring just to a boil and remove from heat. Pour scalded cream mixture over chocolate. Let sit 5 minutes. Stir until smooth. Stir in liqueur. Chill until firm, about 2 hours. Scoop chilled mixture into round balls using a truffle scoop or melon baller. Roll truffles by hand to round and smooth. Place on a lined baking sheet. Chill while preparing coating.

METHOD FOR COATING: Place the chocolate in a double-boiler over low heat. Stir frequently and remove from heat just before completely melted. Stir off the heat until all the chocolate is melted and smooth. Line a baking sheet with parchment or wax paper. Remove chilled truffles from refrigerator. Dip truffles into the melted chocolate using a chocolate dipping tool or toothpick, completely covering the truffle in melted chocolate. Set on lined baking sheet and repeat with remaining truffles. Set aside until firm. Cover and store in a cool place.

Acknowledgements

In researching and writing this book, there were many who offered invaluable help. I would like to give thanks to the management of Royal Palms and Destination Hotels & Resorts (DH&R). I would like to give special thanks to Greg Miller for his steadfast support of this project in both its original and in this newly revised edition. Special thanks also goes out to Nancy Silver, who has been with the property since the redevelopment in 1996 and has helped establish its unique culture, and to Nancy White, who expertly managed the blending of new text and photography.

A sincere thank you is extended to Sally Overgaard, the grand niece of Florence Cooke, and her husband Robert Overgaard for providing new photos and additional rich, historical information about the Cooke family that was made available for this next edition. A special thanks goes out to former owners Fred and Jennifer Unger, of Spring Creek Development, who opened their doors for the first edition and gave me the story behind the restoration. Thanks must also continue to architect Don Ziebell, of OZ Architects, for his early insights and knowledge of the property before, during, and after it was transformed. Thanks must also go to Fred Renker and Robin Renker Eidsmo for their help on research during the hotel's "glamour years." Additional gratitude is owed to former owner Fred Dreier and his daughter, Jill Alanko, for access to their library of historical photography.

I would also like to thank the many people that have helped make this book a reality, including Rich Heineck, Robert Isacson, Cathy Gerstmann, Gwen Walters, Erin Stremcha, Deland Bentz. I want to thank the many interior designers that helped us tell the story of each room. In addition, we want to thank Carrie Miner for her help with the history of Phoenix and Sarah Mandell for her research with participating interior designers.

Robert Z. Chew